Socialist History Society

Treason
Rebel Warriors and Internationalist Traitors

Tobias Abse, Ian Birchall, Steve Cushion, Irena Fick, Christian Høgsbjerg, Jonathan North, Merilyn Moos, Pádraig Óg Ó Ruairc, Irene Recksiek and David Rovics

Socialist History
Occasional Publication 44

SOCIALIST
HISTORY
SOCIETY

Published by
The Socialist History Society, 2019

ISBN 978-0-9930104-9-1

*Front cover illustration: Following U.S. military courts-martial, Irish defectors were executed for treason
and hanged en masse on September 12, 1847.*

Treason
Rebel Warriors and Internationalist Traitors

Introduction - Rebel Warriors

Steve Cushion and *Christian Høgsbjerg*

No more deluded by reaction
On tyrants only we'll make war
The soldiers too will take strike action
They'll break ranks and fight no more
And if those cannibals keep trying
To sacrifice us to their pride
They soon shall hear the bullets flying
We'll shoot the generals on our own side.

The *Internationale*, Eugène Pottier - Paris, June 1871

All men should have a drop or two of treason in their veins, if the nations are not to go soft like so many sleepy pears.

Rebecca West, *The Meaning of Treason*, 1952.

This publication aims to explore a rich, inspiring but very neglected modern historical phenomenon - namely those rare high moments of international solidarity when soldiers not only, in the words of *The Internationale*, "take strike action" and mutiny – but go further and then actually side with (and sometimes defect to and fight alongside) the oppressed, rather than following orders to kill and subjugate.[1] So comparatively rare and short-lived are such moments in modern world history, and often involving few heroic "rebel warriors", as we have termed them, in each such moment, that it is probably too strong to talk of a "tradition" of "internationalist renegades and traitors" here.[2] The possible exception is Ireland, which as we will see seems to have been somewhat exceptional in its internationalism, from the United Irishmen through to the Saint Patrick's Battalion and beyond. Nonetheless, this booklet aims to begin to recover at least some of the better known examples of this phenomenon, both because these "rebel warriors" remain inspiring and offer timely lessons for today in intransigent internationalism and also because until we view this phenomenon across time and place rather than treating each as an isolated incident it is impossible to decide whether we can draw wider lessons or see patterns emerging. One of the very first clear examples in modern history of this phenomenon took place amid the English Revolution or Civil War, which is defined in

1 This booklet arose out of a workshop organised by the London Socialist Historians Group in May 2018 at the Institute for Historical Research. We would like to thank all who contributed and took part, including Keith Flett for his help with the organisation of this workshop.
2 The term "rebel warriors" owes much in inspiration to Asian Dub Foundation's song of that name, originally on their 1995 album *Fact and Fictions*. The song was inspired by the anti-colonialist poem *Bidrohi*, translated from Bengali as "The Rebel", and written by Kazi Nazrul during the 1920s.

many ways as a clash over the very concept of "treason". If one definition of "treason" is "violation by subject of allegiance to sovereign or chief authority of state (e.g. encompassing or intending a sovereign's death, levying war against him, or adhering to his enemies)", then the ambiguity about whether treason related to the "sovereign" or "chief authority of state" went to the heart of the conflict. Was King Charles I or Parliament sovereign?

In January 1649, King Charles I was executed for high treason for conspiring with foreign Catholic powers, after the triumph of Oliver Cromwell's New Model Army, a clash well dramatized in the film *Cromwell* (1970). But that world historical moment, which delivered a powerful blow to the concept of the Divine Hereditary Right of Kings, was also accompanied by another remarkable moment. Later that year, some rank and file soldiers in the New Model Army under the influence of Leveller agitators rebelled against Cromwell's plans to send the army to Ireland. On May Day 1649, a regiment of cavalry in Salisbury refused to proceed and elected Agitators and then their own officers to replace those who had fled the scene. They were quickly joined by other regiments. Two pamphlets circulating in this time reveal some of the arguments at stake. In *The English Souldiers Standard to repair to, for Wisdom and Understanding in these doleful backsliding times. To be read by every host Officers to his Souldiers, and by the Souldiers one to another* (April 1649), it was noted:

> *Whatever they may tell you, or however they may flatter you, there is no less danger lies at the bottom of this business for Ireland, and therefore it behoves everyone of you to lay it to heart: and before you resolve upon a new Engagement, first see a new Representative of the Army established, by the free Election of every Regiment; and refer your selves to their Counsel and advice in all things, to be disposed of as they shall see cause; and neither admit of disbandings, nor of any new listings, nor of any undertaking for Ireland, or any other service, but as that Councell shall advise.*

> *For consider, as things now stand, to what end you should hazard your lives against the Irish: have you not been fighting these seven years in England for Rights and Liberties, that you are yet deluded of? and that too, when as none can hinder you of them but your own Officers, under whom you have fought? and will you go on stil to kil, slay and murther men, to make them as absolute Lords and Masters over Ireland as you have made them over England?[3]*

Another pamphlet, *The Souldiers Demand*, which appeared in May 1649 at the height of the rebellion which would be crushed by Cromwell at Burford, called upon common

---

3 Quoted in Morton, A.L. (ed.), *Freedom in Arms: A Selection of Leveller Writings,* London: Lawrence and Wishart, 1975, pp. 238-239.

soldiers to rise up against their officers, and asked them:

> ...*to observe the cunning fetch they have plotted to send us into Ireland ... what have we to doe with Ireland, to fight, and murther a People and Nation (for indeed they are set upon cruelty, and murthering poore people, which they glory in) which have done us no harme, only deeper to put our hands in bloud with their owne? We have waded too farre in that crimson streame (already) of innocent and Christian bloud ...*[4]

These soldiers and left-wing Levellers left us a classic early example of anti-imperialism and intransigent internationalism at the high point of a revolutionary upheaval, and this booklet aims to explore subsequent similar episodes. In a sense the Levellers' actions fall under the much better known and studied tradition of "mutiny" and the relationship of "popular movements and the military" in general, rather than the phenomenon we are describing, as the Levellers were repressed before any of them could even consider going and fighting in Ireland against Cromwell's army.[5]

There is a wider scholarly literature on "foreign volunteers" who, as defined by Nir Arielli, "leave their country of nationality or residence and take part in a conflict abroad on the basis of a personal decision, without being sent by their government and not primarily for material gain".[6] This might encompass in a sense the phenomenon we are attempting to explore in this booklet, though we are primarily interested here in those who were sent by their government to fight in a particular conflict abroad, but then decided to desert and volunteer to fight for the other side.

More critically, we are not however primarily interested in desertion for desertion's sake, or even in defection for defection's sake, but rather those who deserted for a mix of personal and ideological reasons – and (an even smaller category still) in particular those who decided to do so for reasons of social justice, because they felt that otherwise they would be fighting on the side of the oppressor. We have therefore excluded discussion of those like the Scottish trade unionist and socialist James Thompson Bain. Bain had once fought for the British army against the Zulus in South Africa and had also been stationed in India, but in 1899 he deserted to fight for the Transvaal against the British in the Second Boer War, where he was captured and only narrowly escaped being executed for treason. Since the Transvaal Republic was a racist state and not historically more "progressive" than the British Empire in this respect, we have excluded his experiences from this study.[7]

In a sense the figures we are most concerned with recovering in this volume have some

---

4 Norah Carlin, "The Levellers and the Conquest of Ireland in 1649", *The Historical Journal*, 1987, 30, 2, p. 280.
5 For more on "popular movements and the military", see Mike Gonzalez and Houman Bareket (eds.) *Arms and the People: Popular Movements and the Military from the Paris Commune to the Arab Spring*, London: Pluto Press, 2013.
6 Nir Arielli, *From Byron to bin Laden: A History of Foreign War Volunteers*, London: Harvard University Press, 2017, p. 4.
7 On Bain, see Jonathan Hyslop, *The Notorious Syndicalist: J.T. Bain - A Scottish Rebel in Colonial South Africa*, Johannesburg: Jacana Media, 2004. Our thanks to David Howell for this reference.

parallels with what Arielli calls "substitute-conflict volunteers", who are "sworn enemies of their own government" and "consist of dissidents and political emigres who seek to change the regimes in their home states but have not been able to attain their goal. Instead, they enlist to fight in a war elsewhere in the hope that one victory will pave the way for the one they long for." Notable examples of "substitute-conflict volunteers" include the Polish legion fighting in the French revolutionary armies and under Napoleon, or those black Americans and German and Italian anti-fascists who fought in the Spanish Civil War.[8]

Modern standing armies which continued into peacetime emerged gradually from the fifteenth to the seventeenth centuries alongside the creation of modern states, which came to regulate warfare. Cromwell's New Model Army in a sense was then a revolutionary example of this. The eighteenth century saw European armies grow massively, as monarchs competed with each other and developments in agriculture increased the availability of food for troops, who could also now move around more easily thanks to developments in road infrastructure. Critically, conscription was now introduced and the army absorbed a large number of those whom the rich and powerful found undesirable. As Frederick the Great of Prussia put it, armies were "for the most part composed of the dregs of society, sluggards, rakes, debauchees, rioters, undutiful sons, and the like, who have as little attachment to their masters or concern about them as do foreigners". Press-ganged soldiers, many former peasants, often rebelled and desertion was rife. During the Seven Years War (1756-1763), some 80,000 men absconded from the Prussian army, 70,000 from the French, 62,000 from the Austrian, and to counteract this there were high levels of recruitment of foreigners. As one French general remarked, "each foreign soldier was worth three men, one more for France, one less for the enemy, and one Frenchman left to pay taxes".[9]

The Enlightenment and French Revolution changed all this though, with radicals and revolutionary leaders attempting to end this dependence on foreign mercenaries and instead build an army of citizens, motivated by nationalism and the idea of service rather than monetary gain – alongside the creation of a more meritocratic officer corps rather than one based on social rank and privilege. France became a nation in arms during the French Revolution, and military service became something honoured and celebrated by nationalist propaganda. More critically for our concerns in this booklet, the ideas of liberty championed during the Enlightenment and the wider Age of Revolutions meant once again amid revolutionary upheavals we saw the phenomenon of changing sides, of "turn-coats".

The English radical Thomas Paine's support for the American Revolution against the

---

8 Arielli, *From Byron to bin Laden*, pp. 114-115. On black Americans in the Spanish Civil War, see Danny Duncan Collum (ed.) *African Americans in the Spanish Civil War: "This Ain't Ethiopia, But It'll Do."* New York, G.K. Hall & Co., 1992.
9 Arielli, *From Byron to bin Laden*, p. 16.

British Empire is perhaps the most famous example here. He rallied the American troops with his book *Common Sense* as a true "citizen of the world".

A less well-known figure was the Scotsman John Oswald. Born in Edinburgh in 1760, he enlisted in the British army in 1776 or 1777, reaching the rank of lieutenant. Sent to India in 1781, he was impressed by local customs and traditions, adopting and championing vegetarianism. After returning to Britain, he became a political radical, advocating direct democracy and opposing the hereditary accumulation of land. When the French Revolution broke out, Oswald was thrilled, like Paine, and moved to Paris where he befriended Brissot and more significantly used his military expertise in the service of defending the French Revolution. As Arielli notes, "he raised a battalion and trained it in the use of pikes. In 1793 he died in battle while trying to put down the large scale revolt that had broken out in La Vendée in western France".[10]

Under Napoleon, the use of foreign volunteers for liberty became state policy, indeed as early as 1797 a Polish legion had formed, with the inscription "free men are brothers" on the uniform, and made up of thousands of Polish émigrés and former prisoners of war from the Austrian army. The first legion fought for the French in Italy, and in 1799 a second legion was raised, with the French arguing that "if the coalesced kings deploy vast armies against free peoples, the latter must admit into their ranks all men whom a sublime fervour calls to fight for the sacred cause of liberty".[11] Yet Napoleon by 1801 had ruled out allowing the Polish legion to fight for their own freedom by concluding a treaty with the Habsburg Empire, and from 1802-1803 many Polish legionaries were sent from Italy to the Caribbean colony of Saint-Domingue to help put down what they were told was a counter-revolution underway by the former enslaved under the leadership of General Toussaint Louverture.[12] C.L.R. James notes in his classic history of the Haitian Revolution, *The Black Jacobins*, how in time the French army realised they were actually putting down a genuine revolutionary struggle for liberty and equality and so "went to pieces" and "some soldiers deserted to the blacks", including the famous case when "a regiment of Poles, remembering their own struggle for nationalism, refused to join in the massacre of 600 black soldiers, ordered by Napoleon's brother-in-law, General Leclerc, and later, when the leader of the Haitian independence fighters, Jean-Jacques Dessalines, was reorganising his army, he would call one of his regiments the 'Polish regiment'."[13] The story of these troops and their experience during the Haitian Revolution, possibly the first clear classic

10 Arielli, *From Byron to bin Laden*, p. 34. On Oswald, see A. Owen Aldridge, "John Oswald and the French Revolution", *The Eighteenth Century*, 31, 2, 1990, and Anna Plassart, "A Scottish Jacobin: John Oswald on Commerce and Citizenship", *Journal of the History of Ideas*, 71, 2, 2010.
11 Arielli, *From Byron to bin Laden*, p. 35.
12 Ruth Leiserowitz, "Polish volunteers in the Napoleonic wars", in Christine G Kruger and Sonja Levsen (eds.) *War Volunteering in Modern Times: From the French Revolution to the Second World War*, Basingstoke: Palgrave Macmillan, 2011.
13 C.L.R. James, *The Black Jacobins: Toussaint L'Ouverture and the San Domingo Revolution*, London: Penguin, 2001, p.258.

case in history of the "rebel warriors" we are concerned with, is told by Jonathan North at length in this booklet.

In Ireland, there was also an identification among many with the cause of enslaved black people. The black abolitionist Olaudah Equiano had made an impact when he toured in 1790, and the 1798 rebellion led by the United Irishmen, though brutally crushed, was itself one of the great Atlantic Revolutions of the period. As Kevin Whelan notes, "many exiled United Irishmen had joined maroon communities in Jamaica in 1799", as after "they were 'incautiously drafted into the regiments'", they "promptly fled to the mountains to fight with maroons and French against the British".[14] Peter Linebaugh and Marcus Rediker record the outcome: "after the rebellion of 1798, the slaughter was vast: thirty thousand, far in excess of the number dead in Robespierre's Terror". They cite a description of a letter from Jamaica in 1799, which was sent to Castlereagh, then Chief Secretary of Ireland:

A vast number of United Irishmen, transported from this kingdom, have been landed there, and incautiously drafted into the regiments on that service. As soon as they got arms into their hands they deserted, and fled into the mountains, where they have been joined by large bodies of the natives and such of the French as were in the island. There have already been some engagements between this part and the King's troops: several have been killed and wounded on both sides.[15]

As Kevin Whelan notes, there is clear evidence that many United Irishmen were inspired by the Haitian Revolution, and Toussaint Louverture's leadership in particular:

The veteran United Irishman James Napper Tandy, although based in France, disproved of the ruthless French suppression of the Toussaint insurrection: "We are all of the same family, black and white, the work of the same creator." Toussaint's struggle engaged the attention of the Irish "rhyming weaver and United Irishman, James Orr (1770-1816) of Ballycarry, County Antrim", whose anti-slavery poems included "Toussaint's Farewell to St Domingo" (1805), "The Dying African" (1806) and "The Persecuted Negro" (1809). Another United Irishman, John Swiney, named one of his sons Toussaint in 1808.[16]

Other veterans of 1798 formed the Irish legion, created by Napoleon in 1803, but sadly this was not used to fight for Irish liberty.

Such struggles helped form what Nir Arielli calls the first great wave of "ideological

---

14 Kevin Whelan, "The Green Atlantic: radical reciprocities between Ireland and America in the long eighteenth century", in Kathleen Wilson (ed.), *A New Imperial History: Culture, Identity and Modernity in Britain and the Empire, 1660-1840,* Cambridge: Cambridge University Press, 2004, pp. 232, 234.
15 Marcus Rediker and Peter Linebaugh, *The Many-Headed Hydra: The Hidden History of the Revolutionary Atlantic,* London: Verso, 2000, p. 279.
16 Whelan, "The Green Atlantic", pp. 233-35.

fault-line conflicts that attracted foreign volunteers", as they pitted "liberty" against "tyranny" and so continued the theme discussed earlier relating to the adoption of the cause of "national movements struggling against monarchies and imperial powers that were perceived as stifling liberty". These included the wars of independence in Spanish America, the successive wars between the Ottoman Empire and the Greeks and others in the Balkans, and the wars of Italian unification.[17] With respect to the wars of independence in Spanish America, in Cartagena in Colombia, there stands a monument to those executed by the Spanish Army following the siege of the city in 1816. One of the martyrs was Santiago Stuart from Ireland, just one of many Irishmen who fought with Simon Bolivar for the independence of Latin America.

One very clear example is the *Batallón de San Patricio*, the Saint Patrick's Battalion, which fought as part of the Mexican Army against the United States in the Mexican-American War of 1846–48. Led by John Riley, an immigrant to the United States from County Galway, it was mainly composed of Irish-American deserters from the US Army, although it included Catholics from many other countries as well, plus some black Americans who escaped from slavery in the American South. Here we start to see a pattern which emerges in much of this "treasonous activity", people who feel a higher loyalty than mere patriotism, in this case religion, later socialism and communism. The unit fought at several battles and finally at the Battle of Churubusco, on the outskirts of Mexico City, where more than 70 men were captured by US forces, 50 of whom were hanged and the rest branded on the face with a D for deserter. In 1997, the then Mexican president Ernesto Zedillo said:

> *Members of the St. Patrick's Battalion were executed for following their consciences. They were martyred for adhering to the highest ideals ... we honor their memory. In the name of the people of Mexico, I salute today the people of Ireland and express my eternal gratitude.*[18]

During the American Civil War there was mass desertion on both sides, for a number of factors, but on the Confederate side one in nine would desert, around one hundred thousand men. As Ella Lonn noted, there was a section of the army, particularly mountaineers from the Carolinas, Georgia, and Alabama who "were distinctly out of sympathy with the cause of slavery as the foundation stone on which was built the prestige of their proud neighbours of the lowlands", while others "cherished a real love for the old Union". Deserters from the confederates found refuges in specific haunts and often banded together. Lonn notes how "it became not unnatural for them before long to come together in bands, ranging from twenty to several hundred, organised in military form under colonels, majors, and captains, well equipped with Spenser repeating rifles and an

---

17 Arielli, *From Byron to bin Laden*, p. 39.
18 Jaime Fogarty, "The St. Patricio Battalion: The Irish Soldiers of Mexico", *Voices of Mexico*, April-June, 2000.

apparent abundance of ammunition....The deserters utterly defied the government ... Mississippi offered the remarkable spectacle of deserters presenting themselves at the polls in armed bodies, exercising the privileges though denying the duties of citizens."[19]

Perhaps the high point of rebellion here came with Newton Knight (1837-1922) – portrayed in the fine film *Free State of Jones* (2016) - who in 1863 after deserting from the Confederate army formed the Knight Company, a band of some 125 Confederate army deserters who resisted the Confederacy during the Civil War and formed alliances with free former enslaved people. Local legends tell of Knight and his men forming the "Free State of Jones" in the area in and around Jones County, in South East Mississippi, at the height of the war. Knight's principal reason for desertion was apparently his anger over the Confederate government's passing of the Twenty Negro Law, which allowed large plantation owners to avoid military service if they owned 20 slaves or more. From late 1863 to early 1865, the Knight Company allegedly fought fourteen skirmishes with Confederate forces.[20] Traitors to the Confederate States of America. But most of the supporters of the Union considered the whole project of the Confederacy to be treason. Who is betraying whom? It seems to be a question of where you stand.

Keeping with America, another heroic figure was David Fagen, a black American born in Tampa, Florida around 1875. In 1898, age 23, Fagen enrolled in the 24th Infantry Regiment of the U.S. Army, one of the four black regiments of "buffalo soldiers" and found himself sent to fight in the Philippine-American War (1899-1902) waged by the American Empire against the new independent republic. After arguments with his commanding officers about the legitimacy of the war and the institutionalised racism of the US Army and rejected requests for transfers, on November 17, 1899, Fagen was one of about twenty black American soldiers who defected to the Philippine Revolutionary Army led by Emilio Aguinaldo. Fagen rose to become a captain as a result of his skills in guerrilla warfare, and was described by the *New York Times* as a "cunning and highly skilled guerrilla officer who harassed and evaded large conventional American units". As Vincent Rafael notes,

Clashing at least eight times with American troops from Aug. 30, 1900 to Jan. 17, 1901, Fagen's most famous action was the daring capture of a steam launch on the Pampanga River. Along with his men, he seized its cargo of guns and swiftly disappeared into the forests before the American cavalry could arrive. White officers were frustrated at their inability to capture Fagen whose exploits by now had begun to take on legendary proportions both among the Filipinos and in the U.S. press.

19 Ella Lonn, *Desertion During the Civil War*, Lincoln: University of Nebraska Press, 1998, pp. vi, 4, 66, 70.
20 James R. Kelly Jr, "Newton Knight and the Legend of the Free State of Jones", *Mississippi History Now*, Mississippi Historical Society, April 2009; Victoria E Bynum, *The Free State of Jones: Mississippi's Longest Civil War*. Chapel Hill and London: The University of North Carolina Press, 2001, and Sally Jenkins and John Stauffer. *The State of Jones*. New York: Doubleday, 2009.

Fagen's success also triggered the fear of black defections ...

By 1901, American forces captured key Filipino leaders including Alejandrino and by March, Aguinaldo himself. Filipino leaders tried to secure amnesty for Fagen, but the Americans refused, insisting that he would be court-martialed and most likely executed. Hearing of this, Fagen, by now married to a Filipina, refused to surrender and sought refuge in the mountains of Nueva Ecija in Central Luzon. Branded a "bandit," Fagen became the object of a relentless manhunt, with a $600 reward for his capture, "dead or alive." Posters of him in Tagalog and Spanish appeared in every Nueva Ecija town, but he continued to elude capture...

To this day, it remain unclear what exactly became of David Fagen. His life after the war continued to be as mysterious as his existence before it. But his actions, largely forgotten in the United States, continue to be remembered in the Philippines as that of an African American man who heroically cast his lot with the Filipino revolutionaries to resist the injustice of American imperial designs.[21]

Another less well known, but equally remarkable example, were those British individuals who came to realise the injustice and oppression of British imperial rule in India and so who sided and fought alongside the Great Indian Uprising or Mutiny in 1857. In May 1857 at Meerut, the mutineers were, according to one account, "urged on by a British woman, the widow of a British sergeant, known as 'Mees Dolly' ... she was summarily hanged".[22] As John Newsinger notes in *The Blood Never Dried: A People's History of the British Empire,*

In Delhi a former British sergeant major named Gordon served with the rebels and was captured in September 1857. His fate is unknown. In Lucknow, Felix Rotton and his three sons fought against the British. And there was a widely held belief at the time that Brigadier Adrian Hope had been killed by a British soldier in the rebel ranks owing to his cockney accent and slang when taunting his opponents. There were undoubtedly other 'unofficial Europeans', Britons who lived among and had married into Indian communities, fighting against the British Empire.[23]

The historian and writer Roger N. Buckley, in his novel *Sepoy O'Connor*, implicitly raises the question about the relationship of Irish soldiers stationed in India at this moment in 1857 through the character of Daniel O'Connor who does decide to join the resistance

21 Vicente Rafael, "David Fagen", *The Black Past* (11 February 2007), https://www.blackpast.org/aaw/vignette_aahw/fagen-david-1875/ See also Willard B. Gatewood, Jr., *"Smoked Yankees" and the struggle for empire: letters from Negro soldiers, 1898-1902* (Urbana, University of Illinois Press, 1971) and Michael C. Robinson and Frank N. Schubert, "David Fagen: An Afro-American Rebel in the Philippines, 1899-1901", *Pacific Historical Review*, 44, 1 (Feb 1975), 68-83. Many thanks to Avery Gordon for alerting us to the story of David Fagen.
22 S. L. Menezes, *Fidelity and honour: the Indian Army from the seventeenth to the twenty-first century*, New Delhi, Oxford University Press, 1999, p. 162.
23 John Newsinger, *The Blood Never Dried: A People's History of the British Empire*, London: Bookmarks, 2000, p.83

spreading all around him. As Buckley writes of his novel:

> It is the story of Daniel O'Connor, an Irish catholic who serves in an English regiment in his native Ireland. He chooses voluntary exile in a sepoy regiment in India as a way of escaping the social and political unrest in Ireland, a struggle that may require him to shoot and kill his Irish brethren. O'Connor quickly discovers, however, that India like Ireland is a land grave with the same weight of British colonial oppression. The convulsions of the 1857 War lead O'Connor to see the Indian conflict as a freedom movement that reminds him that his service in the British army is a symbol of the defeated Irish back home. He is faced with a cruel choice should he decide to join the Indian freedom fighters: death or permanent exile in a foreign world.[24]

One Irish figure who we know did choose rebellion, James Joseph O'Kelly, having had to flee to exile in the Americas for his activity in the Irish Republican Brotherhood, fought alongside José Maceo in the Ten Years War for Cuban independence from Spain (1868-1878). On his return to Britain, and while an elected MP in the British House of Commons, he tried to run guns to the Zulus and, in 1884, was arrested by the British Army trying to reach Muhammad Ahmad, known as the "Mahdi", to offer support in the fight for the independence of Sudan.

In general while it appears the Irish who found themselves stationed with the British army in India during 1857 remained loyal to the British Crown, one of those moments when one might expect "rebel warriors" to emerge but they did not, the process of serving in India in the British army would prove a radicalising experience for many in the longer term.[25] Perhaps the most notable example here is Michael Mallin. A rank and file soldier in the Royal Scots Fusiliers, Mallin was sent to India in 1896. His regiment was tasked with suppressing what was called the "Tirah Revolt" - a general uprising in the region close to the Khyber Pass. Mallin wrote frequent letters home to his fiancée in Ireland:

> The war is lasting a very long time dear. We ought to leave the poor people alone for I am sure they will never give in and they have proved brave men God help them. If I were not a soldier I would be out fighting for them ... I wish it was for Erin I was fighting and not against these poor people.

The social injustice and inequality he witnessed there first hand convinced Mallin that

24 See Roger N. Buckley, *Sepoy O'Connor*, Kolkata: Writers Workshop, 2016. This novel is the final part of a literary trilogy by Buckley exploring questions of culture, race, gender, politics identity and nationality in the British colonial army of the nineteenth century using the medium of historical fiction: 'Accommodation and Resistance: Three Chose Rebellion'. *Congo Jack*, Pinto Press, 1997, 'the opening novel in the trilogy, is set in Dominica, the British West Indies, in 1802' and deals with a mutiny by seven African soldiers of the all-black 8th West India Regiment'.*I, Hanuman*, Kolkata: Writers Workshop, 2003, is 'set in British India at the time of the rebellion of the Bengal Army in 1857, it is the true story of Bedasee Singh, a Hindu soldier who is compelled to choose between his loyalty to the British overlord and his devotion to his Indian Motherland'.
25 For evidence of Irish loyalty to the British Empire during 1857 in India, see Joye, Lar. "Irish VCs and the Indian Mutiny", *History Ireland* 18, no. 4, 2010, p. 17.

Ireland must rid itself of British rule. Mallin became an organised socialist and joined Connolly's Irish Citizen's Army on his return, playing a leading role in the Easter Rising of 1916, during which he was executed.[26] During the Irish Revolution and War for Independence which followed from 1919-21, the Connaught Rangers stationed in India mutinied in solidarity with the struggle back at home in 1920.[27]

The Irish have figured largely in our story so far in different ways and have generously contributed to other peoples' struggles for freedom. It is fitting that at least some of this was repaid by British figures, including soldiers in the British Army. Pádraig Óg Ó Ruairc in his contribution to this volume tells of Arthur Wicks, the son of a boot maker from Norwich and member of the Industrial Workers of the World who died fighting in the Post Office during the Easter Rising, as well as the surprising number of soldiers in the British Army who sided with the IRA during the Irish War of Independence.

As we saw with the Levellers who refused to help colonise Ireland during the English Revolution, revolutionary upheavals are sites where one should not be surprised that "rebel warriors" emerge.

The years 1917-1919 also saw many mutinies in imperialist armies, including the French army mutinies of 1917, the German naval mutinies of November 1918 and the French naval mutinies in the Black Sea in 1919.[28] With respect to the Russian Civil War, it remains unclear whether many of the soldiers sent to fight with the White Armies actually switched sides to fight for the Red Army directly, though it is possible there were some French Senegalese troops who did this in South Russia, in Odessa. Though corroborating evidence remains hard to come by, according Vijay Prashad, "some Senegalese soldiers, fighting under the flag of the French empire, decamped for the Soviet Red Army when they heard of its arrival into world history. Boris Kornilov, the Soviet poet, would later sing in his *Moia Afrika* of a Senegalese soldier who died leading the Reds against the Whites near Voronezh 'in order to deal a blow to the African capitalists and the bourgeoisie'."[29]

Many of these questions resurfaced with a vengeance in the period we could call the "Long Second World War", starting with the Nazi seizure of power in Germany in 1933 and ending with violent anti-colonial struggles in the old European Empires. From the 1930s to the 1950s, after the rise of Nazism this period saw Fascist Italy's war on Ethiopia, the Spanish Civil War, the annexation of Austria and Czechoslovakia, the Hitler - Stalin Pact[30] and the partition of Poland, the invasion and occupation of France, Operation

26 Brian Hughes, *Michael Mallin: 16 Lives*, The O'Brien Press, 2013.
27 Sam Pollock, *Mutiny for the Cause*, London, 1969.
28 Ian Birchall, "From Slaughter to Mutiny", *'Stop the First World War'*, London, SHS, 2016, pp.35-48
29 Vijay Prashad, *Red Star over the Third World*, New Delhi: LeftWord Books, 2017, p. 39.
30 Formally known as the "Treaty of Non-aggression between Germany and the Union of Soviet Socialist Republics". Also known as the Molotov - Ribbentrop Pact. It was a neutrality pact between Nazi Germany and the Soviet Union signed in

Barbarossa, the Civil War in Italy, the campaign for Indian independence and the emergence of the Indian National Army, the Battle of Stalingrad, the Anglo-American invasion of Europe, the Warsaw Rising, the Allied Victory and then the start of the new Cold War. All these crises tested national loyalties and political affiliations to the limit, and several contributions to this volume including those by Tobias Abse, Irena Fick and Merilyn Moos, testify to many incredible acts of heroism and internationalism by individuals in the face of mounting barbarism

From the earliest days of the Nazi regime, many working class Germans were quite prepared to conspire with the USSR, the principal external enemy of the legal government of the German nation. This was clearly "treasonous" and as a result Communists, socialists and trade unionists became the first inmates of the new concentration camps. Many managed to flee to France and then became some of the earliest recruits for the International Brigades fighting Spanish nationalist and fascist forces whose main international backer was the same German state of which they had once been citizens. Let us then celebrate the Battle of Guadalajara where German and Italian *Brigadistas* of the Garibaldi and Thälmann Battalions were the spearhead of the defeat of the Francoist forces backed by the Luftwaffe and the entire Italian expeditionary force. Taking up arms against troops of your own nation is the defining hallmark of the "treasonous rebel warriors" this booklet is dedicated to examining.

It is also worth noting that once again we also find Irish people at the forefront of international solidarity, and Christy Moore recorded a tribute to the Irish who volunteered for the International Brigades fighting in the Spanish Civil War:

They came to stand beside the Spanish people
To try and stem the rising fascist tide
Franco's allies were the powerful and wealthy
Frank Ryan's men came from the other side

Even the olives were bleeding
As the battle for Madrid it thundered on
Truth and love against the force of evil
Brotherhood against the fascist clan

CHORUS

Viva la Quinta Brigada
"No Pasaran", the pledge that made them fight
"Adelante" is the cry around the hillside
Let us all remember them tonight.

Moscow on 23 August 1939 by foreign ministers Joachim von Ribbentrop and Vyacheslav Molotov, respectively.

But slowly the Francoist forces wore down Republican resistance and, with the fall of Barcelona, many thousands of republican fighters and their families, including the surviving Germans and Italians from the International Brigade, sought refuge in France where they were interned in French concentration camps.[31] The Hitler - Stalin Pact threw many orthodox Communists into confusion and gave Nazi Germany a free hand to fight on the Western Front. It also infuriated the French government so much that they banned the Communist Party (PCF) and passed a law allowing the death penalty for PCF membership. So the thousands of executions conducted by the German occupation forces and their French collaborators were perfectly legal. This raises the question: "Who was the real traitor? De Gaulle or Pétain?"

The "Fall of France" placed the interned Spanish Republican refugees as well as the German and Italian "undesirable aliens" in a very dangerous position. Many were reported to Nazi Germany where they were killed in the concentration camps; the Nazis had a particular hatred of these anti-fascist fighters. Nevertheless, large numbers managed to escape and with the growth of the rural resistance from 1942, these military-trained militants frequently formed the local nucleus and backbone of the burgeoning rural revolt against Berlin and Vichy. The Spanish Republicans and Italian *Brigadistas* were classic "substitute-conflict volunteers", fighting fascism in France with the intention of returning to Spain and Italy to militarily overthrow the fascist regimes in their homelands, while the Germans were able to directly fight their own fellow countrymen who were occupying France.

There was also an internal resistance to Nazism inside Germany. The generals behind the bomb plot against Hitler of 20th July 1944 are reasonably famous, although their intended peace proposals are less well known; they wanted to maintain most of Germany's territorial gains in Eastern and Central Europe, with the right to continue hostilities against the USSR. Hardly traitors, in fact their supporters refused to cooperate with surviving Communists in the establishment of a memorial to the anti-Nazi resistance on the grounds that they were acting as patriotic Germans while the Communists were betraying Germany to the Soviet Union. Virtually unknown and unsung is the working-class resistance in Germany which Merilyn Moos's chapter justly celebrates and begins the process of rescuing these unsung heroes from what E.P.Thompson called the "enormous condescension of posterity". Workplace sabotage, go-slows in war industries and linking up with foreign forced labourers, were real attempts to undermine the German war machine. And following the arrest of many of these militants, they continued their fight from within the camps.

---

31 As David Rovics put it, highlighting the role of the US, "*The Republic had the people / But the fascists had the tanks / Il Duce and Der Fuhrer / Deserve only some of Franco's thanks / 'Cause the fuel to move the armour / Came from the USA*". See "The Last Lincoln Veteran", from *Big Red Sessions & Ten New Songs* by David Rovics.

Conscripted Communist workers on the Eastern Front initially tried to warn the Russians of the intending invasion and once hostilities had started there were desertions to the Red Army. The 999 Punishment battalion, formed of conscripted Communists and other undesirables, showed a particular tendency to treasonable behaviour that earns them an honoured place in our history of "rebel warriors". But changing sides was not only a feature of the Eastern Front. German Communists in France set up an organisation called *Travail Allemand* (TA) to spread propaganda amongst the occupying troops. It had some success in persuading individual soldiers to desert or supply information to the Resistance, but at the cost of over 100 arrests and executions, mainly of women.

Thousands of Ukrainians, Belorussians and Georgians joined the German Army *SS Ost-Legion* in the mistaken belief that they would win independence for their homelands from what they saw as Russian occupation. Treated with contempt by their racist German officers, many were sent to France to fight against the growing guerilla movement there. This was not what they had in mind when they signed up, so, recognising that they had more in common with the *Maquisards* than with their own officers, thousands of them mutinied and fought with the French Resistance, echoes of the Polish soldiers in Haiti two centuries earlier years. So it was ironic that many then joined the French Foreign Legion and fought against the decolonisation movements in Vietnam and Algeria.

The post-war French Empire got off to a bad start with the Sétif and Guelma VE Day massacres in Algeria leaving 100 settlers and between six and ten thousand Muslims dead. The French wars of decolonisation deeply divided French society, but the interesting aspect from our point of view is the number of French citizens who did more than merely peacefully protest. A courageous group of socialists, Communists, Trotskyists and Christians actively supported the independence forces in both Vietnam and Algeria. A lesson here for the British people who say "I demonstrated against Blair's War in Iraq along with two million others, but it did not stop the war, so what is the point of these demonstrations?" The British *Stop the War* movement lost much support as soon as war was declared and "our boys" were involved. An imperialist ruling class are not going to be deflected by street demonstrations, no matter how large. Rather, they need to see their war effort seriously undermined by activity by the organised working class and that, by definition, is "treason", although socialists may prefer the term "international solidarity". For this reason alone, the story of the French "bag-carriers", highlighted by Ian Birchall in his contribution to this volume, deserves wider circulation.

The decolonisation of colonial settler states always seems more fraught than the decolonisation of colonies of exploitation. Most of the French anti-colonialists who sided with the indigenous population of Algeria and Vietnam were not themselves colonists; Maurice Audin, a mathematician at the University of Algiers who was arrested in 1957, then tortured and murdered, was one of the few Europeans in the country to support Algerian calls for independence.[32] The 1956 Treason Trial in South Africa ended in farce in 1961, but the African National Congress (ANC) moved into the terrain of real treason when they formed their armed wing *Umkhonto we Sizwe* (Spear of the Nation) in 1961. If Nelson Mandela and Goven Mbeki, as men of African heritage, were commonly seen as freedom fighters, Dennis Goldberg and Ronnie Kasrils, both classified as "White", are much easier to see as traitors and were commonly condemned as such by White South Africans. As well as helping found the *Umkhonto we Sizwe*, Kasrils recruited and organised the "London Recruits", which saw British radical students recruited in London undertake undercover activity for the ANC in exile in apartheid South Africa, an ally of Britain.[33] Kasrils is also known for his strong criticisms of the government of Israel and for his sympathies towards Palestinian political struggles. He organised the "Declaration of Conscience by South Africans of Jewish Descent" in 2001 against Israeli policies in the occupied territories. Kasrils raised solidarity between the victims of apartheid states, noting that "Israeli measures to oppress the Palestinian struggle are an intolerable abuse of human rights, so we raise our voices as Jews and cry out, 'Not in my name'."[34]

The decolonisation process was just as bloody for the British Empire, but they were much better at divide and conquer, deliberately engineering a murderous relationship between Muslim and Hindu in India, Turk and Greek in Cyprus or Catholic and Protestant in Ireland, thereby enabling the British Army to appear to be "keeping the peace". One group that managed to overcome these divisions was the Indian National Army (INA) formed by Subhas Chandra Bose during the Second World War, to fight for Indian independence in alliance with Imperial Japan. The INA, mainly recruited from Indian Army prisoners of war and 43,000 strong at its peak, fought alongside the Japanese Army against the British and Commonwealth forces in Burma. The end of the war saw a large number of the INA soldiers repatriated to India where 300 faced trials for treason. These trials had a galvanising effect on Indian nationalist feeling and were an important contributing factor to the Bombay mutiny in the Royal Indian Navy and other mutinies in 1946. Of course it is debatable whether the INA soldiers were traitors and "rebel warriors" with respect to the British Empire or Indian patriots.

In conclusion, in the twenty-first century, the nation-state has become the standard unit of political organisation while nationalism has developed into the fundamental ideology of capitalist society, buttressed by racism, its mirror image. Across the world the (now generally professional) army, the heart of the state machine, has come to embody national

---

32 John Talbott, "The Strange Death of Maurice Audin". *Virginia Quarterly Review*, 1976.
33 Ken Keable (ed.) *London Recruits: The Secret War Against Apartheid*, London: Merlin, 2012. See also the forthcoming film *London Recruits*.
34 "Declaration of Conscience on the Israeli-Palestinian Conflict by South Africans of Jewish Descent", online at https://www.mepc.org/journal/declaration-conscience-israeli-palestinian-conflict-south-africans-jewish-descent

pride, reinforced by all the ideological weapons at the disposal of the ruling class. If the carrot is a feeling of belonging, then the stick is the brutally harsh law against mutiny, desertion and treason. The heroes and heroines of this book, the "rebel warriors" who have placed international solidarity and justice above loyalty to their state and its rulers, deserve to be better known and appreciated; they often paid a very high price for their courage and bravery in leaving this world a better place than they found it.[35]

35 There are doubtless many other "rebel warriors" who deserved to be mentioned and discussed in a volume like this, but which we inadvertently failed to include. The editors would welcome information about such figures and would obviously include them in any future editions of this booklet.

Soldiers of Misfortune: Napoleon's Polish Deserters in the West Indies

Jonathan North

A new republic was born on 1 January 1804. The French colony of Saint Domingue, the western half of Hispaniola, had thrown off a hundred years of French rule to proclaim itself independent. A fierce war had raged for a decade, but had ended in November 1803 with the evacuation of what remained of an army Napoleon had sent to subdue the colony. Now a new regime formed by rebel generals found itself master of a population of former slaves and several thousand French settlers. The following year, after one of the victorious generals had declared himself emperor, and after the majority of the European settlers had been massacred, Haiti was issued with a new constitution. It abolished slavery for ever and declared that Haiti was a free state subject to none other in the universe. But some thirteen articles after these high phrases there was an unusual addition. Article 13 specifically granted rights and privileges and protection to Poles and Germans.

The presence of Poles and Germans in the Caribbean in the early 19th century is in itself rather unusual. But that these men were accorded rights and privileges in the new empire of Haiti is even more surprising. And that they belonged to the French army which had so recently tried to suppress the drive for independence and restore Napoleonic rule makes it even more noteworthy.

Haiti's path to independence had begun with the French Revolution. In France that revolt ushered in a wave of radical reforms. France abolished feudalism, declared a republic, and executed a king. France's Caribbean colonies had to wait a little while for declarations of liberty and equality to be converted into reality but in Saint Domingue, the jewel in the crown of French colonial possessions, the revolution became real on 29 August 1793. On that date slavery was abolished and hundreds of thousands of black slaves found themselves released from slavery if not quite yet from servitude.

Britain, to her shame, intervened on behalf of the former slave owners and stoked a civil war which released a century of racial tension. As the conflict wore on, Toussaint Louverture, one of 8,000 free blacks in the colony, emerged as the leader of an army of former slaves and, by 1798, had driven out the British and their auxiliaries and nominated himself governor general. For now, at least, he kept the colony nominally loyal to France but his victories had flattered his confidence and he was increasingly independent minded. France, beset by continental enemies, had too many troubles of her own to care and so, for now, Louverture was allowed his autonomy.

That laissez-faire approach changed when France finally mastered the European empires through the genius of Napoleon Bonaparte. Napoleon, turning on the revolution that had made him, had assumed power and declared himself First Consul in November

1799. Whilst the first year of his rule was dedicated to asserting central control over France and promoting French power across Europe, his interests were broad and his ambition great. Perhaps inevitably, his vision extended to the restoration of France's rich colonies seeing there the opportunity to restore that flow of revenue the West Indies had once generated and the chance to show that France had returned to its former great power status. When the British started making overtures for peace, Napoleon's attention was free to think of restoring complete control in the Caribbean. Saint Domingue, as the most significant powerhouse of colonial manufacturing, and a colony which could create enormous wealth for a France bankrupted by war, would inevitably play a central part in such an attempt. The colonies would answer directly to Paris and Louverture, or any like him, who thought independence or autonomy was a viable option in a Napoleonic empire, would have to comply or be cast out as rebels. Convinced that all this was possible, Napoleon set about organising a series of expeditionary forces.

His plan was to overawe Louverture's government, and to send sufficient men to deal with any reluctance to be overawed, and impose central control. For now, Napoleon spurned the advice of former colonists and the merchants of Bordeaux that slavery should be restored, calculating, realistically, that such a move would provoke resistance. After all, the First Consul was pragmatic enough to recognise that freed slaves, believing themselves to be enjoying the rights of all Frenchmen, would make better labourers and soldiers than resentful serfs. Perhaps once the colony was pacified the old system, or a new Napoleonic *Code Noir,* could be re-imposed for the good of French commerce.

The expeditionary force concentrated in the French Atlantic ports was no small undertaking and Napoleon, hinting at the importance of the project, had given the task of subduing the colony to his brother-in-law, General Leclerc. It was not a question, as some have alleged, of the First Consul ridding himself of Jacobin elements in his army by sending them to certain death in fever-stricken islands, for Leclerc was placed in command of some of the best troops available.

He and 18,000 Frenchmen set sail on 14 December 1801, and, in February 1802, the French expeditionary force began to land in the colony and was soon securing the main ports – Le Cap Français and Môle Saint Nicolas in the north, Saint Marc in the centre and, eventually, Port-au-Prince, Léogane and Les Cayes in the south. This first wave of troops, predominantly French veterans, although there was one battalion of Germans, met with disaster. The French would be starved, exhausted by constant marching, worn down by disease and decimated by Yellow Fever. And they found that, far from being received peacefully, they faced a guerrilla war from the very start. Leclerc's army met a hostile reception from Toussaint Louverture and his subordinates, most of whom suspected that the Europeans had arrived to restore slavery (as would be the case that July in

Guadeloupe). After a short campaign, Leclerc managed to induce many to return to obedience, and eventually seized Toussaint and sent him to France, but the revolt soon burst forth once again in August 1802 as Yellow Fever destroyed what remained of Leclerc's men. Leclerc himself would die of that disease but the bloody war continued, and escalated, under his successor, General Dontien Rochambeau. The increasingly desperate French were only finally defeated in November 1803 allowing Saint Domingue to declare independence as the Republic of Haiti on 1 January 1804.

Whilst the initial expeditionary force sent to Saint Domingue was predominantly French the reinforcements sent to the island to replace their catastrophic losses included a sizable number of foreigners. Here Polish troops would dominate, some 5,000 of them eventually being sent to the West Indies in two supplementary expeditions (one in May 1802 and one in January 1803).

The Poles sent to Haiti were involved in a merciless war to put down a rebellion by former slaves. Throughout the campaign Polish morale was poor and, as it neared its end, many switched sides to join the rebels.

Such a substantial number of Poles is too much to be a coincidence and it is likely that Napoleon targeted men from the Polish legions. A number of historians have alleged that the new ruler of France wished to rid himself of those who had become tainted by their allegiance to the revolution and that he therefore decided to send these Polish republicans to their deaths. However, as we have seen Napoleon first sent some of his best troops, commanded by his brother-in-law, to the West Indies. However, the suggestion that when he heard that the campaign was to be long and costly he preferred to send foreigners in order to spare French lives carries more weight. This was the case with both the units of German deserters and the Poles, sent in January 1803. By that time Napoleon was aware that the war in the West Indies had gone awry and that the price of conquest was going to be intolerably high. Shrewd statesman as he was, and seeing that a simple conquest had transformed into a costly war of attrition, he was not tempted to risk additional French lives when he had just restored peace to France. In one such example, also in 1803, some 200 French citizens, probably Belgians, who had once served in the Austrian Army and who now, accompanied by "40 or 50 women with 70 or 80 children in the greatest want", were directed to the Atlantic ports. In another he informed his Minister of War that a 700-strong battalion of German deserters, known as the 2nd Foreign Battalion, being readied for service in the colonies "can take in Poles and Swiss and even Italians, and thus this unit can be used to send away turbulent men whose presence might jeopardise the tranquillity of Italy". His loyal Minister of War saw the advantage at once:

The measure will simultaneously ensure tranquillity within the country by sending away men who are rightly suspect, whilst also increasing the strength of the troops in the colonies.[1]

The Poles, with no homes to return to, and many of them having already deserted from one army to another, could be seen as suspect even without taking into account any of their political beliefs. However, sending these restless and unemployed Poles overseas also served an often overlooked political purpose. It resolved an awkward diplomatic situation.

Poland itself had ceased to exist in 1795 following the third partition by Austria, Prussia and Russia. Many Poles fled abroad, and many army officers were inevitably attracted to the enemy of their enemies, republican France. The new republic was glad to find friends. The Jacobins had been suspicious of the Polish nobility and their nationalist cause but their fall, and the arrival *en masse* of thousands of exiles following the final partition, encouraged the French to form distinctive Polish units whose motivation, when sent to fight Austrians and Russians, was without question. So it was that a Polish Legion was operational by late 1796. It was to serve under the then promising young general Napoleon

---

1 The generals in Saint Domingue were less impressed. Leclerc complained that one unit was made up of brigands from Provence, half of whom deserted to the rebels. Whilst a merchant, Morange, noted how "the latest detachment landed and no sooner had it done so than they got drunk and, after being sent to the barracks, they began to fight amongst themselves."

Bonaparte in Italy and it was there that the Polish national anthem was composed by one of its officers. This early unit was raised from volunteers and was soon boosted by deserters from the Austrian army and volunteers from prison camps. Before long there were two legions, numbering 5,000 men, in French pay. Years of hard campaigning in Italy followed with the Poles, many of whom were now nominally Austrian citizens following the partitions, particularly distinguishing themselves against the Habsburgs.

Whilst France was using the Poles for her own purposes, the Poles were, by and large, intent on independence for Poland, and saw service with France as a means to this specific end. Many of the officers were professional soldiers, the sons of middling landowners or impoverished gentry, and were not as radical or as politically active as some of their French peers. Yet, service in the armies of the republic, under the slogans of liberty, equality and fraternity, and imbibing the radical values of militant reason, had an effect and many of the Poles, over time, became firm believers in the cause they were fighting for. What mattered most, for them, was the chance to see those values take hold in an independent Poland.

When a defeated Austria sued for peace many in the legions thought that Napoleon would move to restore their country's independence. However, the peace signed at Lunéville did not even raise the Polish question, and many Poles saw it as a betrayal. Peace also meant that the presence of thousands of Austrian deserters in the French Army became a cause of possible friction between the signatories especially when Austria began to demand that the legions be dissolved and personnel, many of whom were from Galicia and Mazovia, returned to Austria. One solution to avoid such a fate was for the Poles to be assimilated into regular French units, or employed by the new republics in Italy. There was indeed a reorganisation in which the Polish legions would form three demi-brigades each of three battalions. Another name change occurred shortly afterwards, the 3rd Polish Demi-brigade becoming the 113th Demi-brigade and the 2nd Polish Demi-brigade the 114th. But this did not quite solve the problem of Austrian hostility to Napoleon's Polish troops. Leclerc's disaster in the West Indies, however, offered a solution to this diplomatic quandary. Napoleon could send the Poles, supporting Leclerc, sparing French lives and appeasing Austria all in one cynical gesture.

In the event, it was the 3rd Polish Demi-brigade, now dubbed the 113th Demi-brigade, and the personnel granted French citizenship, which had the honour of first receiving orders to march for Livorno on a new and secretive mission in French service. Secretive, rather than secret, for, as Major Bolesta informed General Dąbrowski, "the West Indies is evidently our destination, it suits everyone to talk of our destination as though it were a secret."

What did the Poles make of their new mission? The sources show that there was a mixed response. Piotr Bazyli Wierzbicki set the tone when he stated:

At last, on 14 May 1802, at around midday, the 113th Demi-brigade of infantry received orders to board the ships, The Poles, though with despair in their hearts, transferred into boats and were ferried to the ships and there, resigned to their fate, sat silently with their weapons and in their uniforms on the deck.

But not everyone was resigned to this fate. Many of the young officers viewed, at least initially, their task as an exotic adventure. Józef Rogaliński quipped:

No one knows our destination, we have three months' provisions onboard. It seems that we are sailing to America to see many marvels on the island discovered by Columbus; naked negroes, negresses who throw their breasts over their shoulders, to meet quadroons, griffes and mulattoes, people of colours other than white, to travel over the sea, eat pineapples which are as abundant as potatoes in Europe ...

In 1803 the embarkation of the second detachment, namely the 114th Demi-brigade, also passed without trouble with some of the men, including Second Lieutenant Wójcikiewicz, even relishing the prospect of a new campaign. All this despite the rumours that the first detachment of Poles had been used up and wiped out. He wrote:

Many of us are young and determined, with luck we shall return from Saint Domingue richer than before, indeed were we not destitute we should not be undertaking such a voyage.

However, inevitably, there was some mute resentment that the Poles were now being used as pawns to conquer colonies for France not least because it diverted the Poles from their declared aim of Polish independence. For now, as they embarked and prepared to sail the ocean, many reflected that they were little more than mercenaries. Most felt duty bound not to express this frustration, particularly as they were now, after all, French citizens serving in French regiments. Unsaid too was the fear that their lives in the tropics were likely to be short and brutal. The West Indies was a notorious posting for European troops. The first Poles to be sent knew that the British had lost thousands of men in 1796 and 1797 to Yellow Fever, or other violent disorders of the climate, the second Polish detachment, sent out in early 1803, knew that the Poles who had proceeded them had been destroyed.

Some of the more thoughtful officers reflected on the paradox that they, soldiers supposedly waging war for liberty and equality, were now being sent to return former slaves to, at best, indentured labour and, at worst, a return to slavery as it had existed before the revolution. Michał Sokolnicki, writing from Genoa in May 1802, was outspoken in his anger and expressed his consternation that "those who had fought for liberty and could tolerate no oppressor, shall now go and place free men in chains and make a trade of them".

But still they set sail. The fate of the Poles bore out those inclined to pessimism. The first detachment, sent out in May and consisting of some 2,585 Poles, were embarked at Livorno, and, despite storms and forced inactivity in Spanish ports, some 2,270 men, accompanied by 19 women and four children, landed in Saint Domingue on 6 September 1802 with a few hundred more trickling in later that month. Some 442 went straight to hospital, whilst the regiment found itself broken up and sent to various fronts.

This first wave of Poles was soon used up and destroyed in the brutal war and, on 23 September, two weeks after their arrival, only 966 remained under arms. The following spring Captain Kobylański reported that his unit had been destroyed because "the soldiers here fight every day, they are besieged, left without pay, without clothes, without relief, are on duty for three months, in short, utter disorder". He says that the seven survivors of the first battalion, and the 48 of the third, were absorbed by the French 74th and 31st regiments, respectively.

Back in Europe the remaining Polish officers in French service heard rumours of the fate that had befallen their comrades and were understandably wary that they, too, might be called to fill the expeditionary force's ranks. After having considered sending Józef Grabiński's 1st Demi-brigade to reinforce the Poles, Napoleon eventually determined on only sending the 2nd, now dubbed the 114th Demi-brigade. This decision again reflected Napoleon's preference for sending auxiliaries to wars of little glory, but he was also persuaded that this unit had a tendency for militancy. Not political militancy, but a taint of mutiny largely provoked by the mismanagement of the colonel, Aksamitowski. This unwanted, expendable regiment, now commanded by Tomasz Zagórski, was actually escorted into Genoa in December and embarked, still in their thicker European jackets, for service overseas. This second wave of 2,447 men in wool jackets set off in January 1803. The passage was not entirely unpleasant. A French passenger, Le Roux, remembered how the officers and their ladies, including three lively and friendly Italians, danced on the deck until nine as well as how everyone enjoyed a performance of the Barber of Seville. It helped divert everyone from a long voyage for it was only between 9 and 29 March that the regiment limped into port in Port-au-Prince.

As before, the unit was split into battalions but this time they were all sent south to Tiburon and Jérémie. Chazotte, a French planter serving in the National Guard, saw what became of the Poles:

Two regiments [battalions] of Polish troops in the service of France were landed at Cap Tiburon from the French fleet. Two days after the landing of these two beautiful regiments more than half their number were carried off by Yellow Fever; they fell down as they walked, the blood running out through their nostrils, mouths, eyes;

their bodies turned yellow, they could not move, they were dead.

Józef Zadora of the 114th, wrote home shortly after his arrival in May 1803, and noted that the 113th was no more whilst his own unit was also quickly being destroyed:

I am probably writing for the last time before I die, for just 300 men of the 3rd Demi-brigade remain along with a few officers. All the rest are dead, including your brother who died just a few months after arriving here. I write to you as hope disappears, reproaching myself for my foolishness of having wanted to see the Americas. I would not wish them on my worst enemy and it would be better to remain a beggar in one's own country than to go to make one's fortune in America where there are a thousand diseases and even if you survive them they will not permit you to take any leave, all they do is order you to serve and fight and the blacks, should they catch you, treat you most cruelly. Despite a storm which lasted for six days I survived the voyage by sea and I am fine. I hope I continue to be so I can come back to Europe. That is what I think about night and day.

In the face of such casualties, and in such alien conditions, the experience of being sent to fight in the Caribbean was almost exclusively a bitter one for the Poles. Their French superiors complained that they were prone to drink, an indication of poor morale. Just a few days after their landing, Leclerc informed General Boudet that he was to receive 750 Poles and that he should "prevent these men from hitting the bottle". Some French generals noted a sluggish apathy in combat, phrased as a rather chauvinistic slur that the Poles lacked the élan of their French counterparts. General Pierre Thouvenot was just one to express this rather biased view. He had written shortly after the Poles had landed, declaring that they were "abominably bad for the kind of war we are fighting" and that March he repeated his doubts to General Brunet: "it is impossible to use them apart from placing them in garrisons and it is also risky to do thus unless they are supported by other troops. Desertion to the rebels is not unusual amongst them." His opinion was that "These bulky and apathetic men, strangers to our way of thinking and our language, transported so very far from their homeland, have lost all their will to continue."

When General Rochambeau replaced the deceased Leclerc he also echoed this view. In a detailed report from March 1803, he set out his thoughts that the Poles were not suited to this war in the tropics:

One cannot accuse these foreigners of being cowards, for they stood and awaited death in formation rather than dispersing and acting as skirmishers, but, as they did not speak French, it proved impossible to move them and give them the momentum necessary in such difficult circumstances. Moreover, they are far from agile and find it difficult to march through the hills.

The French therefore determined that these apathetic warriors would be better off protecting ports and plantations than in risking defeat in pitched battle. Such a slight was an additional blow to sensitive Polish honour.

However, along with the trauma of exile to the tropics, and the rather unjust and unhelpful criticisms of their commanders, Polish morale was weakened still further by the nature of the conflict. The attempt to reconquer the colony had slipped into a brutal and barbaric war almost as soon as the expeditionary force landed. By the second half of 1802, as the first wave of Poles landed, it consisted of a series of atrocities punctuated by the burning of towns and villages. The surviving Poles were to witness some of the more horrific massacres. A Polish detachment saw hunting dogs, used to pursue runaway slaves in Cuba, brought in to be used against fleeing rebels or rebel prisoners. On 10 March 1803 a Polish officer in the 114th Demi-brigade called Weygiel informed his friend Nowicki that

War is not the same here as it is in Europe. Three days ago, they bought 200 dogs here from the Spanish colonies. We hope for another 400 tomorrow. They test them on living Negroes and the dogs tear them to pieces and devour them.[2]

Piotr Bazyli Wierzbicki recalled in his memoirs how

When the dogs arrived at Port-au-Prince, they were tested in a trial in which they tore up a black man taken out of jail for the purpose.[3] It should be noted here that at this time the number of prisoners was very large, for those who were only suspected of being in rebellion were imprisoned, and the inhabitants of the city, for reasons of security, had denounced and handed over many of their own slaves to the civil authorities. The strongest of the blacks was then selected from the prisoners, and was brought to the governmental palace which was surrounded by a high wall. Then, in presence of General Rochambeau and his numerous staff, the dogs were released and at the appropriate command the poor victim was torn to pieces on the spot.

The episodes involving the hunting dogs placed the Poles in the position of being onlookers. Some, such as Weygiel, treated the idea of using hunting dogs as an instance of the kind of uncivilised warfare they had to adapt to. But others, such as Ludwik Dembowski, sensed that such atrocities were feeding resistance to French rule. In November 1803 he was sent as a hostage while negotiations with the rebels took place for the evacuation of Le Cap. He was sent to Dessalines' headquarters where

I had the opportunity to meet the leader of the rebels as I was sent to him as a

---

2 A further detachment arrived in June 1803. Morange recalled how "General de Noailles has arrived here [Port-au-Prince] from Havana in a brig loaded with horses and dogs."

3 This probably refers to the notorious incident at Le Cap when dogs were tested on one of General Boyer's guides.

hostage for 24 hours. Despite their apparent savagery they treated me well and despite our notion that they were ignorant they do reason rather well in their own way. Amongst other things, they seemed to want to convince me that they were obliged to take up arms against us for, otherwise, they could not be sure of their continued physical or moral existence. They cite lots of blood spilt, an infinite number of their compatriots drowned or shot all because of some vague suspicion, thousands banished without motive, and, finally, death sentences without there ever having been a fair process to check these arbitrary acts. Such barbarous acts rallied brave men to the cause of the rebels, individuals who knew only the word liberty even though their own liberty had been granted to them by the French government, or the Committee of Public Safety, as they deemed it.

If the Poles had been onlookers to many massacres, at least one other incident, and one more massacre, has the Poles involved in the butchery. This was an incident on 17 October 1802, and it is important as, although it seems as though the Polish troops were participants, the horror their officers expressed resonated with the rebels the French were fighting and earned them, as unwilling executioners, a certain sympathy.

This atrocity took place at Saint Marc when a battalion of the 12th Colonial Demi-brigade, nominally in French service, but suspected of getting ready to go over to the rebels, was massacred on a parade ground. Although it seems that the 71st and 79th Line were the key perpetrators of the massacre, Polish troops were also present even though there is some confusion as to their precise role in the events.

The assassination of the black battalion took place on the orders of General Leclerc. These were issued on 16 October, just as the insurgents were attacking Cap Français. The French later justified the massacre on account of them lacking sufficient troops to secure black units of dubious loyalty. The sequence of events was as follows: When the orders to kill the blacks reached General Fressinet he conferred with his immediate superior, General Quantin, and they resolved to muster the colonial troops on the Place d'Armes at Saint Marc. They were to parade without their weapons. Walking in front of the troops, Fressinet delivered a harangue to the effect that he was declaring them traitors to France, lifted his sabre and gave the command to his European soldiers to bayonet the blacks to the last man. According to Polish sources, the Poles complied, and did not question the orders. Many even seem to show some sympathy for Fressinet's decision, writing that there was no alternative to murdering these unarmed soldiers, as it would be impossible for the Poles to guard such a large number of prisoners. Piotr Bazyli Wierzbicki saw the massacre as a military necessity:

It was impossible for our single battalion to detain a few hundred blacks in captivity, so there was no alternative but to exterminate them to the last man. Coming to this conclusion, and seeing that it called for bold and prompt action, General [Philibert] Fressinet, our commander, ordered a roll-call of the black men to, to be performed, as was the custom, without weapons. When they were standing on the square, the battalion under Major Bolesta, surrounded them unexpectedly and killed them with bayonets.

However, a pre-eminent 19th century Haitian historian presents an entirely different version of events. According to Madiou, "the Polish troops had fought with little enthusiasm against the indigenous forces since attempts had been made to re-establish slavery. They proudly declared that only military duty could induce them to burn their gunpowder against freedom." And so it had nothing to do with the massacre. Another historian, Beaubrun Ardouin, goes even further and implies that the Saint Marc massacre might well have been the defining moment for Polish-Haitian relations. He states that Dessalines, from that point on, spared the Poles for

He had a reason to spare them as, quite recently, when the 12th Demi-brigade was massacred at Saint Marc, the Poles had shown considerable repugnance at the barbarity of General Quantin.

The truth probably lies somewhere in the middle. The Poles may have taken part in the massacre but subsequently showed revulsion and disgust, perhaps even regret. It was enough for the rebels to be able to discern a difference in attitude between the French soldiers and their reluctant auxiliaries. It was a difference they exploited.

When the tide turned against the French, those Poles who surrendered in the south certainly seem to have met with relatively good treatment whilst their French comrades in arms received short shrift. Piotr Bazyli Wierzbicki explained how

Later, when the blacks learned how we were sent to Saint Domingue, they changed their conduct towards us and henceforth began to treat our prisoners with greater humanity. Paul Louverture, commander of the local blacks, once had those Poles who had been taken prisoner brought before him, and he offered that they remain in Saint Domingue as free men enjoying all civil rights.

The rebel officer Geffrard had allowed the surrender of Polish troops at Anse-à-Veau and sent them to Dessalines, who kept them at Michel, and some of these also seem to have taken up rebel service. Poles taken at Jérémie when General Fressinet loaded his French troops onto merchant ships and abandoned his Polish detachment in the citadel were also spared and many ended up settling on plantations in the area. A detachment at Dame-Marie would also surrender but only after its commander, Ignacy Jasinski, blew out his brains after having informed his superior that "I am no longer in a position to hold out with such a small detachment, and I do not wish to fall into the hands of a savage people so evidently fighting for their liberty". The officer's 50 men were taken alive and soon blended in to the local population.

As well as those surrendering to the rebels, some Poles, perhaps inevitably given the approaching disaster, voluntarily switched sides. Admiral Latouche-Treville had already protested to Paris that too many foreigners were being sent to the colony and that it was not clear whether sending these men "of dubious morale was intended to assist the army or merely provide recruits for the brigands". As we have seen, General Pierre Thouvenot, also thought the Poles were prone to desertion. It is certainly true that the rebel commander Ferrou, a man of considerable humanity, coaxed some of the Poles into his service and it was rumoured he was commanding a unit of Poles and Germans by the spring of 1803. Dessalines also had a unit of Poles. This is borne out by Polish accounts too, for, according to Darewski, writing back to Poland on 16 August 1803, some "30 fusiliers from our 3rd Demi-brigade had gone over to the rebel side and they now form his [Dessalines's] personal guard". This seems confirmed by other sources which state that when Dessalines, who, as we have seen, showed a certain empathy for the Poles, crowned himself emperor in 1804, his throne was protected by a unit of Polish and German guards. In another instance, General Pamphile Lacroix states that the rebel Clervaux had managed to persuade a hundred or so Poles to desert and that he had even them mounted on horses to form a kind of rebel cavalry. Lacroix was understanding, as he had also felt the paradox of fighting rebel soldiers who sang the Marseillaise and other republican hymns as they went into battle. We cannot be sure of the exact number of such deserters, perhaps there were 200 or so, but, as a proportion of the Poles who survived the disaster, this was a sizable minority.

Polish historians have been relatively keen to downplay this aspect of Polish participation in the war in the West Indies. At the time Polish officers were similarly wounded by any suggestion that their men could be anything other than loyal. A number suggested that the French were slandering their countrymen in order to use the Poles as scapegoats by the French to excuse the loss of the colony. Kazimierz Małachowski, who survived the campaign, was, on his return to France, astounded to hear that senior generals had been leaking to the newspapers suggestions that the Poles had betrayed their allies. As he put it:

Here I should probably mention something which now occurred, which damaged the character and the honour of the Poles, and, truth being a requirement of history, I wish to set the record straight. Captain Żymirski, who reached Paris before us, learned of my arrival in Bordeaux and wrote me a letter, informing me that the French newspapers, and, shortly afterwards, the foreign press, had published the news that the Poles had deserted to the Negroes and were now fighting against the

French. This was the excuse for the colony not being able to resist. Distressed by such news, I decided to go to Paris to raise the matter.

Polish officers, supported later by a number of Polish historians, naturally denied or diminished the instances of desertion, but also sought solace in the notion that it was only the rank and file who deserted, and that no officers went on to serve in rebel ranks. There were some officers whose fate was not known, who did not escape from the island, and it is possible that some of them remained voluntarily as the French departed.

This brings us to the final aspect of the Polish experience, and the one with which we began. What became of the Poles who had surrendered or deserted to the rebels after the French defeat, and why were they afforded special privileges? In all some 500 were left in the colony when the French troops were evacuated and, of these some 400 volunteered to be naturalised as citizens. This was understandable as in the months following independence there were several large-scale pogroms of white settlers, particularly in the south.

By the end of February 1804 some 400 Poles had signed the act of naturalisation in which they "manifested their wish to be inscribed in the permanent register of those constituting the residents of the island of Haiti." They also swore that they

Following the French defeat, the rebels of Haiti dealt harshly with any Frenchmen they laid hands on. The Poles were, in contrast, accorded special protection under the new constitution.

would "never again serve against us on the side of the French but would, on the contrary, defend us". The act of naturalisation then ended with a rather unique form of words for the time, namely that "we declare with the present act that we count Citizen X as being one of the children of this island and, recognising him as such, desire and command that all the other inhabitants recognise him as such and that therefore Citizen X, regardless of the different colour of his skin, shall enjoy the same rights as those of the natural inhabitants of this place."

When Dessalines, that violent friend of the Poles, proclaimed himself emperor, his administration presented Haiti with a new constitution which made special reference to the naturalised Poles and Germans. Their rights to live and own property were, in contrast to those of other Europeans, particularly the French, were to be specifically protected by Article 13 of the constitution of independent Haiti. These naturalised citizens seem to have settled in to life in their new empire. A few of the Poles were, however, less keen on enjoying their hard-won privilege. Several tried to escape. British accounts mentioned picking up isolated detachments of Poles along the Haitian coast in early 1804, such as when Edward Corbet informed Governor Nugent of Jamaica that:

> *One reason for trading at Jérémie on our return here was partly to take onboard such of the Polish troops remaining in that quarter as chose to volunteer for our service …. Captain Perkins [of the Tartar] had some time since procured permission from the General-in-Chief. They were so scattered in different dependencies that only 11 could readily be found.*

Others went through official channels and, in the spring of 1804, 160 Poles asked Dessalines for permission to be returned to Europe. They boarded the Tartare and were first taken to Jamaica where the British, instead of sending them to Europe, tried to incorporate them in the depleted 60th Foot. They refused and were returned to Haiti. There they were placed on the Ontario, an American merchantman, and were eventually shipped to New York and on to Copenhagen in late 1805. Although a further 15 would quit the colony in 1807 the rest, perhaps some 300 to 400 individuals, remained and, for better or worse, attempted to make Haiti their home.

Some served in Dessalines' army or worked at the gunpowder mill at Marchand the capital, dubbed Dessalinesville but abandoned after the assassination of the new emperor. Most seem to have worked the land, but evidence is lacking and we see only glimpses of what became of the Poles who remained before a revival of interest in Poland itself, and the development of anthropology, led to some Polish scholars taking up an interest in studying their descendants. By the 1960s studies on the light-skinned and grey-eyed inhabitants of the village of Cazales in the west and the town of Port Salut in the south west were appearing. The survival of surnames such as Lipinsky, Adelsky and Voycyk or the more generic Polak showed the degree to which the Polish legacy had endured. And it is still present today.

Aside from that legacy, what, then, is the significance of this rather obscure episode in European and Caribbean history? I would suggest it is one of symbolism for communities on both sides of the Atlantic. For the Haitians the presence of Poles affirms the righteousness of their cause during the revolution. Prisoners and deserters came to their banners to support that cause and ranged themselves alongside the former slaves. The episode is also symbolic for Poles too, or at least the wider story of the destruction of the

Polish legions is. That cynical destruction, when a European power betrayed the Poles for their own selfish ends by sending them to almost certain death, fed into yearning for independence throughout the 19th century. It was a sacrifice which reinforced the notion that only independence from the manipulation of great powers could prevent Poles from becoming pawns in some great game. Only independence for Poland could guarantee a future for the Poles. The loss of 5,000 of Poland's best was just one more station along Poland's way of the cross. But there is a complication when it comes to looking specifically at the men who chose to remain in Haiti.

The Poles who surrendered and settled in Haiti, as well as those who deserted the French and sided against them, find themselves in an uncomfortable position historically. On the one hand they affirm a tendency amongst Polish nationalist historians to insist that Poles, wherever they fought, and whomever they fought against, were always on the side of liberty. On the other hand they contradict that other tendency, articulated by the same set of historians, to suggest that Polish soldiers were always loyal and reliable troops. These 400 individuals challenge such a generalisation. And for that reason, as well as some of the real difficulties involved in following this bizarre episode, the Poles of Haiti have largely disappeared from the historical record.

Further Reading

This text is drawn from my introduction to *War of Lost Hope: Polish Accounts of the Napoleonic Expedition to Saint Domingue, 1801 to 1804* (London, 2018), co-authored with Marek Tadeusz Łałowski, and which presents four first-hand accounts by Polish officers sent to the West Indies. There are a number of good French and Polish studies providing the historical context of the French expedition to Haiti, but the best English-language account is Philippe Girard's *The Slaves Who Defeated Napoleon: Toussaint Louverture and the Haitian War of Independence* (Tuscaloosa, 2011). It is very detailed, deftly examines the issues and uses archival material to trace the course of the campaign. There are just a handful of English-language studies on the neglected Polish participation in the conflict and the best is still Jan Pachonski and Reuel K. Wilson's *Poland's Caribbean Tragedy: A Study of Polish Legions in the Haitian War of Independence 1802-1803* (Columbia, 1986), even though it relies heavily on Kazimierz Lux and Peter Bazyli Wierzbicki's narrative. Although rather difficult to find, I would recommend the 1986 thesis by Nicole Darne-Crouzille. Her *L'Expédition Leclerc-Rochambeau à Saint-Domingue* (Le Mans, 1986) includes letters by Polish participants found in the partially destroyed General Dabrowski archive in Warsaw. Finally, regarding those Poles who remained behind following the French surrender, I do not think that Tadeusz Łepkowski's "La présence polonaise dans l'histoire d'Haïti et des Haïtiens" in *Estudios Latinoamericanos* (11, 1998) can be bettered.

The Saint Patrick's Battalion

David Rovics
(*Living in these Times,* 2001)

The Saint Patrick Battalion War Memorial in
Ciudad de México

My name is John Riley
I'll have your ear only a while
I left my dear home in Ireland

It was death, starvation or exile
And when I got to America
It was my duty to go
Enter the Army and slog across Texas
To join in the war against Mexico

It was there in the pueblos and hillsides
That I saw the mistake I had made
Part of a conquering army
With the morals of a bayonet blade
So in the midst of these poor, dying
Catholics
Screaming children, the burning stench
of it all
Myself and two hundred Irishmen
Decided to rise to the call

From Dublin City to San Diego
We witnessed freedom denied
So we formed the Saint Patrick Battalion
And we fought on the Mexican side,
We formed the Saint Patrick Battalion
And we fought on the Mexican side

We marched 'neath the green flag of Saint Patrick
Emblazoned with "Erin Go Bragh"
Bright with the harp and the shamrock
And "Libertad para Mexicana"
Just fifty years after Wolfe Tone
Five thousand miles away
The Yanks called us a Legion of Strangers
And they can talk as they may

But from Dublin City to San Diego
We witnessed freedom denied

33

So we formed the Saint Patrick Battalion
And we fought on the Mexican side,
We formed the Saint Patrick Battalion
And we fought on the Mexican side

We fought them in Matamoros
While their volunteers were raping the nuns
In Monterey and Cerro Gordo
We fought on as Ireland's sons
We were the red-headed fighters for freedom
Amidst these brown-skinned women and men
Side by side we fought against tyranny
And I daresay we'd do it again

From Dublin City to San Diego
We witnessed freedom denied
So we formed the Saint Patrick Battalion
And we fought on the Mexican side,
We formed the Saint Patrick Battalion
And we fought on the Mexican side

We fought them in five major battles
Churobusco was the last
Overwhelmed by the cannons from Boston
We fell after each mortar blast
Most of us died on that hillside
In the service of the Mexican state
So far from our occupied homeland
We were heroes and victims of fate

From Dublin City to San Diego
We witnessed freedom denied
So we formed the Saint Patrick
Battalion
And we fought on the Mexican side

A bust of John Riley in San Jacinto Square,
Mexico City

Deserters, Defectors and "Diehards" - The British men who fought and died for Irish Freedom

Pádraig Óg Ó Ruairc

The centuries' long struggle against British imperialism in Ireland has often been misrepresented in over-simplistic nationalist terms of English coloniser versus Irish native or framed as a sectarian religious struggle between Protestant and Catholic. The truth of course is that Irish history and politics are far more complex and nuanced. The philosophy of Irish Republicanism was inspired and heavily influenced by the French Revolution and when the philosophy first developed in the 1790s the leadership of the United Irishmen, who fought to establish the first independent Irish Republic, were primarily Protestants and Presbyterians descended from English and Scottish colonists. At the same time native Irish Catholic clergy were amongst the staunchest supporters of Monarchism and British rule in Ireland.

Irish Republicans were always willing to seek support from British radicals sympathetic to their cause. In the 1790s they were in contact with their Republican counterparts in the Society of United Scotsmen and the United Englishmen. Later they had links with the Chartists, the labour movement and British Marxists. Perhaps the most vocal and public expression of this came in 1867 when the Irish Republican Brotherhood, more commonly known as "The Fenians", issued a proclamation during their short-lived revolt which declared an independent Irish Republic and in the same breath voiced their spirit of revolutionary internationalism:

We declare, in the face of our brethren, that we intend no war against the people of England. Our war is against the aristocratic locusts, whether English or Irish, who have eaten the verdure of our fields – against the aristocratic leeches who drain alike our blood and theirs. Republicans of the entire world, our cause is your cause. Our enemy is your enemy. … Workmen of England remember the starvation and degradation brought to your firesides by the oppression of labour. Remember the past, look well to the future, and avenge yourselves by giving liberty to your children in the coming struggle for human liberty.[1]

At the turn of the 20th century all of Ireland was an integral part of the United Kingdom yet the overwhelming majority of the Irish population yearned for independence from Britain and had pinned their hopes on "Home Rule" - an extremely limited form of self-government within the United Kingdom and British Empire. However, even this meagre political concession to the Irish only enjoyed only the lacklustre support of the British Government who indefinitely postponed the Home Rule Act in the face of opposition from

---

1 Excerpt from the 1867 Proclamation of the Irish Republic which is worth reading in full. Similar Proclamations were issued by John Sheares during the 1798 rebellion, Robert Emmett in 1803 and during the 1916 Rising. For a lecture by the author comparing these visit: www.youtube.com/watch?v=AX919bJJ_IM&t=1873s

conservative British Army officers in England and the Unionist minority in Ireland. The resulting political crisis brought the remnants of the Irish Republican Brotherhood, members of the Irish Labour movement, suffragists who other radicals together, and in 1916 they conspired to launch an armed uprising to establish an independent Irish Republic. As well as establishing an independent Irish Republic the 1916 Rising was also an attempt at a social and political revolution, a clash between Republican and Monarchist politics and not merely a struggle between rival nationalisms. Unsurprisingly hundreds of Irishmen served in British uniform during the short-lived revolt and forty-one of them died fighting for the English King and the British Empire whilst suppressing the rebellion.[2] Likewise, a few dozen of the rebels who took part in the revolt were from Britain. Most of them were of Irish ancestry, but one, an English Socialist killed fighting for the Irish Republic, had no previous connections to the land of his death.

Arthur Wicks was the son of a boot maker from Norwich. He worked in the hotel industry, joined the Industrial Workers of the World in 1911 and later played a key role during the London Hotel Strike of 1913 for which he was imprisoned. Following his release Wicks found it impossible to get employment as he had been blacklisted for his trade union activities. In 1915 he moved to Dublin and using the alias John Neal he managed to get a job as a waiter in the upmarket Shelbourne Hotel. In due course he lost this job after getting involved in the Irish labour movement and he had to find new employment at the Hotel Allen on Dublin's Harcourt Street. Wicks joined the Irish Citizen Army, a workers' militia led by Edinburgh born Republican-Socialist James Connolly. The legend surrounding Wicks's enlistment is that

Arthur Wicks

when this earnest but unknown Englishman presented himself as a potential recruit at Citizen Army Headquarters in Liberty Hall stating he had conscientious objection to fighting for a capitalist - imperialist government in his homeland, but that he also had a conscientious objection to being left out of a fight for liberty in Ireland, he was duly accepted as a member of the force.[3]

When the 1916 Rising began, Wicks, known to his Citizen Army comrades by his alias

2 For more details see: Richardson, Neill, *According to their lights – Stories of Irishmen in the British Army, Easter 1916*, Dublin, 2016.
3 *The Irish Worker's Voice*, 19th April 1930

Neale, participated in the demolition by explosives of the Great Northern Railway viaduct at Fairview which was intended to delay British Army troop trains from reaching Dublin city centre. Afterwards Wicks was stationed at the Republican headquarters in the General Post Office (GPO) and he was then transferred to the Metropole Hotel garrison on the opposite side of Dublin's main thoroughfare Sackville Street. On the fifth day of the fighting the garrison of the Metropole Hotel was forced to retreat back to the GPO. During their retreat a rebel alongside Wicks was struck by a bullet which caused an ammunition pouch he was wearing to explode. Wicks bore the brunt of this suffering shrapnel wounds to the thigh.

Wicks's comrades dragged him to safety and carried him with them on a stretcher as they continually retreated from the advancing British forces during the final twenty four hours of the revolt. Following the surrender of the Republican forces a British soldier noticed Wicks among the rebel prisoners lying wounded on a stretcher laid on the pavement. This soldier unbound Wicks's bandages causing him further blood loss and his condition rapidly deteriorated. The military ordered that Wicks be moved to a British Army field hospital at Dublin Castle; however he died that night in the castle courtyard lying on a stretcher still awaiting medical treatment.[4]

Although the 1916 Rising was quickly suppressed by the British forces, the Republicans' protest in arms awakened in the Irish populace a desire to fight to secure their full rights as free men and women rather than accept the political table scraps of Home Rule offered to them as subjects of the British King. In the 1918 General Election the Irish people voted in overwhelming numbers for the new Sinn Féin party whose candidates stood for election on the basis that if elected they would not take their seats in Westminster but would instead establish an independent Irish parliament in Dublin – Dáil Éireann. The result was a landslide victory for the Republicans who won 73 of the 105 Irish seats in the House of Commons compared to just 25 Unionist MPs and 6 Home Rule MPs. On 21st January 1919 Dáil Éireann met for the first time. It issued an Irish "Declaration of Independence" and issued the "Democratic Programme of the Irish Republic", which outlined the rights and freedoms of the Irish people including the nationalisation of all state wealth and resources, the provision of medical care and social protection for the poor and the protection of workers' rights.[5] The British Government moved quickly to supress the rebel assembly and the conflict that followed, known as the Irish War of Independence, pitted the resolve of Republican Ireland against the might of the British Government, its Empire and armed forces.

At the same time the Irish Republican Army (IRA) had begun waging a military campaign against the British Forces in defence of the Irish Republic. During that conflict

4 Jimmy Wren, *The GPO Garrison in Easter Week 1916 - A Biographical Dictionary,* Dublin, 2015, pp. 374 -75.
5 The Democratic Programme of Dáil Éireann, 21st January 1919.

the British Government maintained a garrison of up to sixty thousand troops[6] and IRA Volunteers continually encountered British servicemen who were perturbed by the oppressive and anti-democratic duties they were charged with in Ireland. In many cases these soldiers wished simply to desert, return to Britain and resume civilian life but occasionally others were found to have developed sympathy with the plight and aspirations of Irish people and were willing to actively help the IRA.

In County Clare for example one local IRA officer William McNamara found that members of a British Army cavalry regiment stationed in Ennis were willing to give material support to the IRA. He was initially approached by two soldiers through a chance encounter during which they expressed a desire to desert. McNamara paid them £8 for their two rifles with one hundred rounds of ammunition and provided them with civilian clothes to help aid their return journey to Britain. However the pair returned to Ennis shortly afterwards seeking McNamara. "A few days later I was in the bar having a drink with Michael Kennedy, when the two of them came in accompanied by five other soldiers. They at once recognised us and introduced us to their pals who, they said, were also anxious to desert." The republicans duly offered them the same deal. "These soldiers were nearly all Scotsmen and the cavalry regiment to which they belonged was used as a 'flying column' moving through the country a good deal. They were a decent body of men and the vast majority of them did not relish the particular class of soldiering at which they were employed in Ireland. On pay nights, when a good number of them got a bit tipsy, they could be heard in the pubs in Ennis singing Irish rebel songs."[7]

The only reason that the former IRA leader, Ernie O'Malley, survived the conflict was due to the assistance of a British sympathiser: Private Ernest Roper from the 2nd Battalion of the Welch Regiment. During the war O'Malley, a regional organiser for IRA headquarters, had been captured by British troops tortured and imprisoned in Kilmainham Gaol, Dublin. O'Malley and two other leading IRA officers, Frank Teeling and Simon Donnelly were facing execution by hanging when Roper helped them escape: "The Welsh military police in charge of the jail had been told we were murderers. That meant an image from a Sunday newspaper of a thug with twitching hands and a furtive walk. But they heard us laugh and sing, joke and refuse to take prison regulation seriously. ... Gradually they learned to talk to us, to laugh and they joked with us about arrests and hangings ... They sat in our cells to enjoy our forbidden cigarettes and they smuggled in half-pints to a few. ... They taught us some of their songs and bits of regimental tradition. We taught them our songs and ballads."[8]

6 Ó Ruairc, Pádraig Óg, *Truce, Murder, Myth and the Last Days of the Irish War of Independence*, Cork, 2016, p. 51.
7 William McNamara, Bureau of Military History Witness Statement - Irish Military Archives (BMH WS 1135).
Ernie O'Malley, ed. by Ó Comhraí Cormac,*The Men Will Talk To Me Galway Interviews by Ernie O'Malley*, Cork, 2013, pp. 278 - 84.
8 Ernie O'Malley, *On Another Man's Wound*, Dublin, 2008, pp 286 – 312.

O'Malley heard that Roper was willing to help the IRA and he approached him: "I met him in my cell. He seemed sincere. I gave him a note for the IRA Chief of Staff and I got a reply from IRA Headquarters. Next I sent a sketch map of our prison wing out and outlined our escape plan." Roper smuggled a bolt cutter into the prison so the IRA escapees could break through a prison gate and he also provided them with a revolver so they could fight their way out if necessary. During the first escape attempt Roper had left the cells of the IRA prisoners unlocked but the trio found that the bolt cutter did not work. The would-be escapees were beginning to question if they were being set up - but Roper was determined that the second attempt would succeed and on the night of 21st February 1921 he himself accompanied the trio to the prison gate and cut the lock with a new bolt cutters and the three duly escaped not only from the prison but also the hangman's noose. Roper and a second soldier, Private J. Holland an Irish Protestant from Belfast, were both tried and convicted of helping the prisoners escape and were sentenced to eight years imprisonment.[9]

With the loyalty of some serving British soldiers in Ireland in doubt it is unsurprising that the British Government were eager to keep Irish regiments in the British Army as far from Ireland as possible. By 1920 every Irish Regiment in the British Army was posted overseas but even that could not prevent the spread of protest and sympathy for Republican ideals within their ranks. On the 28th June 1920, a company of the Connaught Rangers stationed at Jullundur in India refused to perform their military duties as a protest against the activities of the British Army in Ireland. On the following day, the mutiny spread to another company of Connaught Rangers at Solon. The soldiers there joined the protest and the Connaught Rangers Mutineers at both barracks lowered the British Union flag and replaced it with the green, white and orange tricolour of the Irish Republic. The Mutineers wore tricolour rosettes on their British Army uniforms and sang Irish rebel songs.[10]

These protests were initially peaceful, but on the evening of the 1st July a group of the Solon Mutineers attempted to seize rifles from their barracks magazine. The sentries guarding the magazine opened fire killing two soldiers. Following this incident troops from the Seaforth Highlanders were deployed to crush the mutiny. One of the leaders of the mutiny James Daly was executed by firing squad and the remaining sixty mutineers were imprisoned. Amongst them was an Englishman - Sergeant James Woods from Bristol. Due to his nationality Woods came in for particular abuse from the soldiers who crushed the mutiny and one officer taunted him saying: "You are an Englishman, what has Ireland got to do with you?" Woods told the officer; "These men fought with me for England, now I am fighting with them for Ireland." As a punishment Woods was kept

9 Niamh O'Sullivan, *Every Dark Hour – A History of Kilmainham Jail*, Dublin, 2007, pp 130 – 134.
10 For more see: Sam Pollock, *Mutiny for the Cause: the story of the revolt of Ireland's "Devil's Own" in British India*.

without food and water for the next two days. Despite this he continued to support the protest. Wood's and his fellow Connaught Rangers Mutineers were imprisoned until the 3rd January 1923. After his release despite being a decorated veteran of the First World War Wood's was unable to find employment in Britain due to his record of support for the Irish cause. He eventually moved to Ireland in the hope of finding employment. [11]

The minority of British soldiers sympathetic to Republican ideals did not always stop at offering material support and solidarity with the Irish people - a number of serving British soldiers defected to the IRA and took up arms for the Irish Republic and the rights of the Irish people. Perhaps the most famous of these was a Scottish soldier known only by his nom-de-guerre "Peter Monahan" who died fighting for the Republic on the 19th March 1921 at the Battle of Crossbarry. Monahan, a member of the Royal Engineers attached to the Cameron Highlanders, was stationed at Cobh just east of Cork City. He became troubled by the actions of the British Army in Ireland and in late 1920 he deserted from his regiment along with a second soldier named Tommy Clarke who was apparently less interested in the rights and wrongs of the military situation in Ireland and was just fed up with army life. The pair got disoriented and after wandering about cold and hungry for several days they wound up in Kilmacsimon Quay. The pair were soon arrested by the IRA who suspected them of being spies and their captors were intent on executing them when Monahan revealed his Republican sympathies. Monahan also revealed that he had worked as a mining engineer in Scotland and had a good knowledge of commercial explosives. This probably saved their lives as the West Cork Brigades efforts at making landmines for attacks had all been unsuccessful. Monahan joined the Kilbrittan Company of the IRA's West Cork Brigade and made mines that were used in several IRA attacks. Clarke remained in hiding with the assistance of the IRA and worked as a farm labourer on local farms until the end of the conflict. [12]

On one occasion when Monahan was leading a small group of IRA volunteers down a country road near Carhoon, Bandon when they met a Loyalist farmer, Thomas Bradfield driving a pony and trap. Bradfield struck up a conversation with Monahan and upon hearing his Scottish accent assumed that the armed men were British troops in "mufti". Bradfield asked Monahan "Is it safe for me to be talking to you, sir?" Monahan replied that it was and Bradfield duly told them the whereabouts of an IRA hideout he had discovered, and continued: "I'm not like the rest of them round here at all. The Reverend Mr. Lord (an Anglican Minister and British Intelligence agent) is my man and I give him information. You fellows should come round and I'll show you around." Having blown his cover and exposed himself as a spy Bradfield was taken prisoner and executed.

Monahan was killed during the Battle of Crossbarry – the largest military engagement

11 Kathleen Hegarthy Thorne, *Echoes of Their Footsteps: Volume 2 The Irish Civil War*, Ohio, 2016, p. 146.
12 Jeremiah Deasy, Irish Military Archives, Bureau of Military History Witness Statement (BMH WS 1738)

of the entire conflict. Approximately 100 IRA Volunteers mounted an ambush in the village of Crossbarry in the hope of ambushing a mobile patrol of British soldiers from the 1st Battalion of the Essex Regiment. The Republicans launched a successful attack on a motorised British Army column and succeeded in killing ten British soldiers. Shortly after the initial IRA attack five hundred British reinforcements descended on the ambush site to encircle the attacking IRA force. Despite being outnumbered and outgunned by their foe the Republicans managed to escape but in the process lost three of their comrades including Peter Monahan. Monahan had been operating the detonating plunger of an explosive mine at the ambush site when he was shot and mortally wounded by the British troops.[13] Monahan's body was recovered by his IRA comrades and buried with full military honours in the Republican plot at Saint Patrick's Church, Bandon. Monahan's real name was never established by his IRA comrades and his tombstone bears his *nom-de-guerre*.

Given the hugely negative press that events in Ireland were receiving in both domestic and international newspapers, the British Government were loath to rely on the British Army as the main bulwark against the IRA during the War of Independence. Sole reliance on military force to supress the insurrection would have been tantamount to admitting that the IRA was a legitimate army. To solve this political problem tens of thousands of recruits, mostly ex-British soldiers, from Britain, Ireland and across the Empire were recruited into the Royal Irish Constabulary (RIC) – Britain's colonial police force in Ireland. These recruits, nicknamed "Black and Tans" were effectively a military force but because they were technically policemen it allowed the British Government to present the Irish War of Independence as a "peace-time" domestic policing action to supress a criminal gang of thieves and murderers.

Following their deployment in Ireland, the "Tans" quickly earned a well-deserved reputation for assassination, murder, torture, arson and the mistreatment of both civilians and Republican prisoners. Even amongst the hated Tans there were a handful of Republican sympathisers. One of these, Leonard Booth, might be considered a "conscientious objector". Booth, a Canadian veteran of WWI, joined the Tans on the 24th August 1920 and resigned almost immediately after his deployment to Ireland. The RIC register recorded his reason for resignation as: "In sympathy with the Irish People".[14] An English "Black and Tan" Basil Somers defected to the IRA and fought for the Irish Republic for several months until he was captured at Wolfhill, County Laois.[15] Another unidentified "Tan" tipped off the IRA that a large motor convoy could be ambushed at Dunkitt in County Kilkenny. When the convoy drove into the ambush position the same Tan called out to his comrades "Stop boys. They are too many for us!" whereupon he and

---

13 Liam Deasy, *Toward's Ireland Free*, Cork, 1973, pp. 236, 242 -3.
14 Royal Irish Constabulary Register – Microfilm Collection, Irish National Archives.
15 Michael J. Rafter, *Laois the quiet County: The Laois IRA and revolutionary activity within the county 1913 -23*, Naas, 2005, p. 133.

the other British troops immediately surrendered their vehicles and weaponry to the IRA without a fight.[16]

The Irish War of Independence came to an end in July of 1921 when the British Army agreed to a formal military truce with the IRA and the British Government agreed to enter formal political negotiations with Dáil Éireann. In December 1921 "The Anglo-Irish Treaty" was signed between the British Government and representatives of the rebel Irish Government. This treaty partitioned Ireland into two states; Northern Ireland which would remain part of the United Kingdom, and the Irish Free State which would secede from the United Kingdom and be granted Dominion Status within the British Empire. The British King would become head of state for the Irish Free State and an oath of loyalty to him was required by members of the new Free State Government. Not only did this political settlement divide the island of Ireland into two, it also split the IRA into two factions. Those who supported the Treaty with Britain became known as the "Free State Army" whilst those who rejected the treaty and wanted to hold out for a fully independent Republic in Ireland retained the title "IRA" but were labelled with the pejorative term "Diehards" by their pro-Treaty opponents. In early 1922, just after the British Government began removing its troops from the Irish Free State and redeploying them in Northern Ireland the Irish Civil War broke out in the south of Ireland between the Free State Army and the IRA. Throughout this new conflict, a handful of British men continued to fight and die for the ideal of an Irish Republic.

Charles Chidley, a veteran of the First World War from Medway in Kent, served in the West Kent Regiment at Crinkle Military Barracks in County Offaly during the War of Independence. Chidley worked as a military driver chauffeuring senior British Army officers and he began passing scraps of intelligence information he gleaned from these British officers to the IRA. On the 28th February 1922, just as the British Army was withdrawing from southern Ireland, Chidley and another soldier, Private George Mines from London, deserted to join the IRA. Chidley was captured by the Free State Army in the autumn of 1922 and interned. The local IRA leader, Sean McGuinness recalled that Childey was fearless in battle: "Chidley served with the local IRA Active Service Unit and played the part of a great soldier when surrounded and riddled with bullets by Free State Troops at Brittas Castle in August 1922."

After recovering from his wounds Chidley was held under armed guard at Portlaoise Hospital, but was later interned in Portlaoise Prison after he launched an unsuccessful escape bid. He was eventually released from prison at the end of the Irish Civil War in March 1923 and returned to England. In 1950 he married Dorris Jones at Bootle Lancashire and he died in 1975. Chidley's comrade George Mines remained in the IRA

16 Terence O'Reilly, *Rebel Heart: George Lennon Flying Column Commander*, Cork, 2009, p.168.

after Chidley's capture and was himself captured after participating in an ambush at Rahugh, Westmeath in October 1922. Following his release from prison at the end of the Civil War Mines moved to Canada but returned to Britain in the 1950s.[17]

One of the most intriguing of the British volunteers who joined the IRA was Ian McKenzie who hailed from Inverness-shire in the Scottish Highlands. McKenzie's father was a Major in the British army and after Ian's older brother was killed in action in France in 1916 his mother moved to Killarney, County Kerry in the hope of saving Ian from conscription and the same fate. McKenzie spoke Scots Gallic and had little difficulty in conversing with native Irish Gaelic speakers. In 1918 McKenzie moved to the Gaelic speaking district of Ballingeary to study Irish and quickly integrated into the local community. One of his Irish friends, journalist, Geraldine Neeson described him as "A most attractive person whom we all liked very much. An extrovert with a consuming curiosity about people and their motivations. He had a sharp, frequently-used wit and a clear, infectious laugh, and was excellent company." McKenzie's main role in the IRA during the War of Independence appears to have been the manufacture of improvised grenades and the procurement of arms and ammunition. In early 1921 McKenzie travelled to England to buy arms for the IRA and returned with eleven new Webley .45 revolvers.

At the outbreak of the Civil War McKenzie cycled from Ballingeary to Cork to defend the city against the advancing Free State Army. On the 8th August 1922 the city fell to the Free State Army and McKenzie and two of his comrades, Frank O'Donoghue and James Moloney were part of an IRA column that was retreating under fire when their vehicle broke down at Belmont Cross. The trio jumped from their lorry and took up position in Belmont Cottage to cover the retreat of their comrades. After a prolonged fire-fight the trio in the cottage were running low on ammunition and having delayed the enemy long enough to facilitate their comrades escape the three decided to surrender. McKenzie opened the door and put up his hands in a token surrender, but both he and Moloney were shot dead. O'Donoghue was captured and taken prisoner. McKenzie is buried in the Republican Plot of St. Finbarr's Cemetery in Cork City.[18]

Ian McKenzie

17 Charles Chidley Pension Application – Irish Military Archives
18 *Irish Democrat* 8th September 2006.

43

Wilfred Bennett a twenty year old Private in the Battalion of the Loyal North Lancashire Regiment who was stationed at Ballyvullen Barracks in in Tralee defected from the British Army on the 31st October 1921 and joined the IRA along with Private Robert Markland a veteran of the First World War from Liverpool. Markland, known to his local Republican comrades as "Little Titch", relieved the British Army of a Lewis machine-gun and several pans of ammunition when he defected and presented these to the IRA. Markland was eventually taken prisoner by the Free State Army on the 10th January 1923. One of the Free State officers holding Markland prisoner had known him during the War of Independence period and asked him what he had done with the Lewis Gun. "Ah, I only had it for shooting crows" was Little Titch's nonchalant response as if he was discussing an antiquated shotgun rather than a valuable piece of military hardware, sorely missed by the British Army and equally coveted by both the Free State Army and IRA alike. His flippancy earned him a prolonged beating from his captors. Markland was held prisoner in Mountjoy Prison Dublin before being released a few months later following the cessation of the Irish Civil War.[19]

Perhaps the most famous British deserter who defected to the IRA was Walter Stenning - alias Reginald Hathaway. "Hathaway" was in-fact Private Walter Stenning of the East Lancs Regiment. Stenning, born in 1903, was from Willesden, Middlesex, England and had enlisted in the British Army just after his 17th birthday in April 1920. After deserting from the British Army in May 1921 he joined the IRA. Immediately prior to the Civil War Stenning enlisted in Free State Army, but this was a ploy to secure arms. Stenning immediately went AWOL taking with him a Lee Enfield rifle and a hundred rounds of ammunition which he promptly delivered to the IRA. A few months later Stenning was captured by the Free State Army and he managed to escape execution by signing the "release form" a document declaring that the signatory had formally surrendered and would never again take up arms against the Irish Free State. But Stennings immediately re-enlisted in the IRA and served with them until he was captured after a three day siege at Clashmealcon Caves. Stenning was executed by a Free State firing squad on the 25th of April 1923. He is buried in the Republican Plot at Rahela Graveyard, County Kerry.[20]

Those mentioned above are just a few of the more prominent examples of the British men who fought and in some cases died for the Irish Republic during the Irish Revolution of 1916 to 1923. Honourable mention could also be given to Private Thomas Johnstone who deserted from the Kings' Own Scottish Borderers in Cork in April 1921 to join the IRA, Private Allan Daw of the Royal Warwickshire Regiment who was stationed in Northern Ireland in 1922 and deserted his post on the border to join the IRA or a number of other unidentified British men who like them who took up arms to fight for the Irish

19 For more see: Tim Horgan et al (eds) *The Men Will Talk to Me – Kerry Interviews by Ernie O'Malley*
20 Tim Horgan, *Dying for the Cause – Kerry's Republican Dead*, Cork, 2015.

Republic but sadly only the barest details of their exploits have survived. As the people of Ireland approach the centenaries of both the Irish War of Independence and Civil War we should reflect on the sacrifice of these British men who risked their lives so that future generations of Irishmen and Irishwomen might know freedom.

Sketch of Arthur Wicks from An t-Óglach April 1926 - 10th anniversary 1916 rising edition

Resistance to the Nazis within the German workers' movement from 1933

Merilyn Moos

Introduction

It is a commonly held myth that there was little resistance in Germany to the Nazis. In fact, there was a wide diversity of opposition to the Nazi state. Although in no way wanting to detract from the bravery of the other people and groups involved, this chapter will focus on the organised resistance from within the workers' movement.

Almost all the resistance groups within the broad workers' movement that attempted to organise collectively were in one way or another associated with the German Communist Party, (KPD). The resistance to the Nazis prior to 1933 was essentially split between the KPD and the Social Democratic Party (SPD), though there were a few active small splinter groups. The leadership of the SPD fled into exile when the party was forced to disband in 1933. At first, they theoretically established an underground organisation but the level of arrests led the leadership to conclude that underground activities were too dangerous and that the regime could only be overthrown by a military defeat. Thereafter, the SPD regularly expelled members critical of their "passivity". There is no evidence of any SPD underground group based in the workers' movement, although there were a few outstanding anti-Nazi individuals, some of whom survived by fleeing abroad.[1]

Unlike in France or Spain, internal resistance to the Nazis was not armed and with a few extraordinary exceptions did not make use of force. The Nazis from the very beginning operated a campaign of terror, the level of repression was extreme: almost every anti-Nazi in this history was murdered by the state. Because of the regular focus on the murder of Jews, the Nazis' visceral hatred of the left, with which both Himmler and Hitler were obsessed, is often overlooked.[2]

The Reichstag fire of February 1933 provided the Nazis with a wonderful excuse, though it is one they may well have helped design. Within three days of the fire, about 5,000 Communists were arrested; in March and April alone, 40-50,000 political opponents were taken into "protective custody" (internment without trial).[3] By June 1933, more than half of the KPD district leaders were in detention. On 2nd May 1933, the Nazis banned the German free trade unions, occupied their premises and packed countless trade unionists off to the concentration camps. Significant members of the Social Democratic leadership were also detained.

The SA/SS trashed town halls, publishing houses and party and union offices and hunted down political and personal enemies. The focal point was Red Berlin but the

---

1 Detlev Peukert, 1987, *Inside Nazi Germany*, London, B.T.Batesford
2 Nikolaus Wachsmann, 2015, *A History of the Nazi Concentration Camps*, London: Little, Brown.
3 Ibid.

SA/SS did not just come for the leading revolutionaries but also for members of a diverse network of sports clubs, artistic circles, humanist and cultural groups all linked with the KPD. All were seen as "terrorists". Up to 200,000 political prisoners were detained in 1933. Indeed the first camps were constructed for Communist prisoners where hundreds lost their lives just in 1933. Between 1933 and 1939, thousands of Communists were arrested; by 1945, about 150,000 had been detained in camps, about half of the KPD membership, and 30,000 executed.

A few examples: Ernst Thälmann, the leader of the KPD, was arrested on March 3rd 1933, three days after the Reichstag fire, and he was shot in 1944; John Schehr, who headed the KPD after Thaelman's arrest, was himself arrested in November 1933 and murdered together with leading Berlin Communists Erich Steinfurth, Eugen Schönhaar, and Rudolf Schwarz, probably in February, 1934.[4]

The mass extermination of Jews has diverted much of our attention from these earlier priorities of the Nazis. From the start, the Nazis were committed to breaking working-class organisation and rooting out Marxism. What is remarkable is that there was any organised resistance from within the working-class movement.

The resistance falls into two broad periods: a few years following 1933 till repression decimated the resistance, and from the outbreak of war, especially from after the end of the Hitler - Stalin Pact.[5] Once war began, the Gestapo (the secret police) and the justice system became even more determined to stifle opposition, a repression which intensified when it began to appear that Germany could be losing.[6] In the last years of the war, the Nazis murdered civilians without bothering with any bourgeois legalities, for as little as listening to the BBC. They murdered concentration camp prisoners, especially left-wing opponents, in increasing numbers as defeat loomed. Resistance to the Nazis had become exceedingly dangerous and highly fragmented, organised into small, isolated units. It is in this context that working-class resistance to Nazism needs to be understood.

I suggest that those involved were certainly perceived as traitors by the Nazis and by many onlookers. Indeed, the chance of getting killed as an active anti-Nazi was higher than being in the German army. As for the few who deserted the armed forces or 'joined the other side', considered briefly at the end of this chapter, they were still seen as traitors by many Germans well after the war had finished.[7]

The role of the KPD as an organisation

Members of the KPD became the leading anti-Nazis in the underground and it is

4 The German Resistance Museum. https://www.gdw-berlin.de/en/recess/biographies.
5 Peukert, *Inside Nazi Germany*
6 Wachsmann, *History of the Nazi Concentration Camps*
7 Lars Peterson, *Hitler's Deserters*, Fonthill Media, 2013.

estimated that about half the 300,000 KPD members took part in illegal activity.[8] But the KPD was not ready for illegal activity in 1933 and had a threadbare underground network. Their ability to offer any leadership was made worse by their political line, which saw the Social Democrats as "Social Fascists". Matters were made worse by the KPD refusal to recognise that they had suffered a major defeat; with one or two exceptions, the members of the Central Committee (CC) did not expect the Nazi regime to last. The last issue of their paper *Die Rote Fahne*, published on the 27th February 1933, states that the swastika will not be victorious and that the working class and the communists will triumph. This fighting mood in part encouraged the bravery of the underground but also made it more reckless.[9]

The KPD was banned in 1933 after the April elections. At the end of March 1933, the Politburo finally decided that the open presence of almost all the leaders of the KPD in Germany had become too dangerous and that the leadership had to go underground. From autumn 1933, of the leadership of the KPD who were still alive and free, almost all were in exile: the External Politburo was based in Paris, with responsibility for organising, printing and smuggling in *Die Rote Fahne* and anti-Nazi leaflets. The External KPD HQ moved in 1935 from Paris to Prague, and then to Moscow, when the centre in Prague also had to close upon invasion. John Schehr, who was the only member of the Party leadership to stay in Germany, was initially the key to organising underground work but was arrested in November 1933 and executed in February 1934.[10]

Too many of the leadership continued to act as if they didn't understand the level of danger they or their members were in. For example, the KPD CC met openly in the home of a comrade three days after the Reichstag fire where the police arrested them all. The KPD decided that its members should try to stay in Germany, not to flee. It was only after *Kristallnacht* or the 'Night of Broken Glass' in November 1938 that this line changed. By 1935, of 422 KPD leaders, 219 had been arrested, 14 killed, 125 had fled and 10 had left the party.[11]

Another problem was that communication between the KPD CC, the Comintern and German resistance groups was dangerous and close to impossible. Local KPD activists were left rudderless and easily picked up by the Gestapo. It was only after the 1935 Comintern conference in Brussels that the reality was recognised and it was decided to move towards localism but most organised groups by then were in a state of collapse.[12]

8 Allan Merson, *Communist Resistance in Nazi Germany* London: Lawrence and Wishart ,1985
9 Mason, Tim, 1995, "The Containment of the Working Class in Nazi Germany", in *Nazism, Fascism and the Working class*, Cambridge.
10 Merson, *Communist Resistance in Nazi Germany*
11 Hartmut Mehringer, 1997, *Widerstand und Emigration. Das NS-Regime und seine Gegner*. München: Deutscher Taschenbuch-Verlag.
12 Merson, *Communist Resistance in Nazi Germany*.

Up to the outbreak of World War 2, there was no clear KPD line to build underground activity. Even then, it is not until after the German invasion of the Soviet Union on June 22nd 1941, that the Communist line changed from the period of the Hitler - Stalin pact. After that, illegal work was expanded, for example illegal leafleting went up threefold between the beginning and end of 1941, but so did the level of arrests.[13]

German resistance groups

There was an appalling arrest and death rate and so resistance groups were inevitably fluid with the same people moving between networks. Despite all that, certain patterns do emerge. Again and again the membership of these groups was mostly industrial workers of some form, though there are relatively few women. Though the professed aim of most of the resistance groups was sabotage and the go-slow, especially in armaments factories, we know more about what was professed rather than carried out.[14] The groups operated on the usual principles of clandestine work where only one person was responsible for and knew about one task, though there seems to have been informers in almost every group.

This article does not go into the debate about the contours of industrial resistance, but more workers than is usually supposed seem to have been involved in industrial, even if not explicitly political, resistance.

Though most of the groups are formed after 1939, at least one resistance group was established before the outbreak of war: the important Uhrig group. Born in 1903, a toolmaker and active member of the KPD, Robert Uhrig was first arrested by the Gestapo in 1934, having edited an underground newspaper and organised collections for the families of people in prison. Sentenced to hard labour, he was released in summer 1936, found work as a skilled craftsman in the Osram electricity works in Berlin where he began to build an underground group. He led a network of underground resistance groups in over 20 factories with around 200 members in Berlin, especially Siemens. After 1939, Uhrig, amongst others, published the underground paper, *Informationdienst* (Information Service), which endeavoured to report on the economic and military situation and called for acts of sabotage. His was an almost entirely working class group, who generally supported the USSR and were committed to establishing a socialist state. Uhrig's was one of the largest resistance networks which continued after 1939 and he was regarded as the leadership of the Berlin KPD.[15]

After the Nazi attack on the USSR in June 1941, Uhrig worked hard to make contact with sympathisers and other groups. For example, in September 1941, he incorporated a group led by Walter Budeus which had members in the Berlin armaments factory

---

13 Ibid.
14 See introduction to bibliography
15 German Resistance Memorial Centre: https://www.gdw-berlin.de/en/recess/biographies/index of_persons;
Eric Brothers, 2012, *Berlin Ghetto. Herbert Baum and the Anti-Nazi Resistance*, The History Press.

Deutsche Waffen und Munitionsfabrik. By the beginning of 1942, Uhrig had links with 89 factory groups. Key contacts included Herbert Grasse, a printer, and Otto Grabowski who had already organised cells in some Berlin factories. He also managed to forge contacts with other communist resistance groups in Hamburg, Mannheim, Leipzig and Munich in the hope of building a nationwide resistance movement that could take on the Nazi state.

One pamphlet, published in mid-December 1941, has survived. It states its purpose is to educate political fighters, it reviews the military, economic and political situation and calls for sabotage and go slows. He, along with Wilhelm Guddorf, John Sieg, Martin Weise and Jon Graudenz, all former KPD editors, amazingly also produced about 400 copies of the clandestine newspaper *Innere Front* in 1941 concentrating on undermining Nazi lies, analysing the military situation and predicting the probability of Nazi defeat.[16]

Uhrig worked with some extraordinary comrades: Beppo Romer, had been an active member of the *Freikorps* who had fought against the Ruhr workers in March and April 1920, but by 1932 had become an organiser for the KPD. He plotted an assassination of Hitler in 1934, was arrested and executed in 1944; Werner Seelenbinder, a wrestler and KPD member who, in 1933, refused to give the Nazi salute when receiving his medal at the German Wrestling Championship. He was punished with a sixteen-month ban on training and sports events but was allowed to participate in the 1936 Olympic Games. He acted as a courier, but was arrested in February 1942, along with 65 other members of the group. He was beheaded with an axe on 24th October 1944. Ernst Knaack, a leading KPD militant in Berlin, arrested in 1935, was detained for two years and then rearrested on 26 March 1942, and executed. Paul Schultz-Liebisch, a decorative painter and KPD member, in 1944, was drafted into the *Wehrmacht* but managed to desert, and Charlotte Eisenblätter who was involved in the Workers' Sport movement, and was arrested in February 1942, sent to Ravensbrück Concentration Camp and killed there on 25th August 1944. By 1941, the Gestapo had infiltrated the *Innere Front* group and in February 1942, Uhrig and 200 other members were arrested. Uhrig was sent to Sachsenhausen and guillotined in 1944.

Although there is insufficient space to look in detail at resistance within the camps, in Sachsenhausen, Berhard Bästlein, who had won a seat for the KPD in the Reichstag election of March 1933, met a number of other comrades and started to build a resistance organisation. In 1937, Bästlein was among the authors of the *Sachsenhausenlied* (Sachsenhausen song), which came into being on the orders of the SS camp commandant, Weiseborn, as the camp song but such was the enthusiasm of the prisoners, it was subsequently banned. Robert Abshagen, who had been active in the *Rotfrontkämpferbund* (Red Front Fighters), joined in in December 1941 as did Franz Jacob and Gustav Bruhn. It is ironic that many of the leaders of the different resistance groups originally met in the

16 Merson, *Communist Resistance in Nazi Germany*

camps.

The group consisted of Communist Party members, some Social Democrats, along with independents and foreign forced labourers. Through extensive contacts, from the winter of 1941, they were able to build a conspiratorial network in over 30 firms, primarily in the Hamburg shipyards, developing over 30 factory cells and supporting prisoners of war and forced labourers, many of whom had been put to work in the shipyards.[17] There was alone an established resistance group of about 100 in the Blöhm & Voss shipyards. Robert Abshagen initially managed the illegal group in the *Vereinigte Deutsche Metallwerke* (United German Metalworks).[18]

Concentrating on large Hamburg companies, the plan was to help promote the overthrow of the regime and end the war. Like other anti-Nazi groups, their goals were broad and open to different political positions. They wanted to maintain a network of anti-Nazi propaganda, educate and mobilise workers, give aid to fugitives from the Gestapo and to forced labourers and prisoners of war, and organise sabotage as far as possible, especially in weapons production.

In the middle of 1942 there was the only known instance of major leafleting, aimed at Hamburg construction workers who had been compulsorily committed in the spring of 1942 to the construction of the "Organization Todt" in Norway and the Soviet Union.[19] The leaflets linked demands for wages and severance pay with the call to commit acts of sabotage. It closed with the slogan, "Hitler's defeat is not our defeat, but our victory!"

However, in May 1942, disastrously, two party representatives, who had flown from the USSR and parachuted into Germany, unwittingly led the Gestapo to the Hamburg group. More than 100 of their then roughly 200 members were arrested and 60 sentenced to death.

Escaping from Plotsensee prison in January 1944, Bästlein helped create an illegal network of the *Bewegung Freies Deutschland* (Free Germany Movement) in Berlin-Brandenburg and published the illegal magazine, *Die Innere Front* (The Internal Front). Then, following a betrayal in 1944, over 280 members of the organization were arrested of which 104 were killed. On 30th May 1944 Bästlein and his comrades Franz Jacob and Saefklow were once again arrested and sent back to Sachsenhausen and executed on 18th September 1944.

Another group in Hamburg with which Bästlein had contact was *Fighting Fascism* (KdF group), led by machine master Carl Schultz and the metalworker Heinrich Schröder, which was cross-class as well as including forced labourers and prisoners of war employed

---

17 Merson, *Communist Resistance in Nazi Germany.*
18 http://www.stolpersteine-hamburg.de/
19 Ibid.

in Hamburg factories. Towards the end of the war, air protection officers and members of the Volkssturm were also included. They operated using clandestine methods in Hamburg Electricity Works and AEG (General Electric Company). From 1944, the group wanted to start to collect weapons, with an eye of the arrival of the Allies. Almost all the group were put to death in April 1945 in Neuegamme camp.[20]

After the arrests in Hamburg on October 1942, Franz Jacob was involved in setting up a resistance organisation with Anton Saefkow, a mechanical engineer, who had joined the KPD in 1924, and had been arrested in April 1933, and released after two years. In 1943, Jacob established a new network of cells in factories with illegal workers groups. This organization, with a membership of about 500, was one of the biggest. Their emphasis was not propaganda but sabotage and impairing arms production. They made a point of contacting foreign workers, both to build a broader base and to offer them aid. The plan was to build a united front with anti-fascist circles, including Social Democrats and the middle class. The group included not just workers, but doctors, teachers, engineers and artists. Unusually, about one-quarter of the members were women. The largest factory group of the organization was at Teves, a machine and tool manufacturer, with about 40 members out of roughly 2,400 employees. Bästlien, Jacob and Saefkow were executed on 18 September 1944.[21]

Finally let us examine a group who represent a synthesis between Communist and Jewish resistance, the Herbert Baum group, who organised one of the few acts of social sabotage.[22]

Herbert Baum

Herbert Baum saw himself primarily as a Communist; his Jewishness does not seem to have been his primary source of identity.[23] From the age of twenty, Baum was the head of the German-Jewish youth group *Ring-Bund Deutsch-Jüdischer Jugend*, joining the *Kommunisticher Jugendverband Deutschlands* (Communist Youth Federation, KJVD) in 1931. The KJVD committee was run by Baum, Ansbach and Steinbrink. Active in the KPD underground movement after 1933, he was a link with Jewish youth organisations. For example, he persuaded Heinz Birnbaum, a turner and a member

20 https://de.wikipedia.org/wiki/Kampf_dem_Faschismus
21 Merson, *Communist Resistance in Nazi Germany*
22 Brothers, *Berlin Ghetto*
23 Rosenstock,Werner, 1974 "The Jewish Youth Movement" in Baeck, Leo, *Institute Year Book* 19.

of the Zionist youth movement, to become a member of the KJVD. Together with Irene Walther, Birnbaum created an illegal cell of the KJVD at the Butzke & Co plant where he worked. He was sentenced to death in 1942, aged 23.[24] In 1934, the Baum group leaflet-bombed Nazi events on a couple of occasions but so many of the people involved got arrested, that they decided it wasn't worth it. But they continued to leaflet factories, warning against exploitation of workers and monopoly capital. From 1936-39, they ran couriers to Prague. Their main work was in seven sports clubs with other red sports clubs clustered around them.[25] In a way unfamiliar to British audiences, the sports clubs in Germany often were frequently affiliated to either the SPD or the KPD.

After the collapse of Hitler - Stalin Pact, Baum wrote that the underground is on the verge of creating a mass movement which will transform an imperialist into a civil war and that they were on the offensive. They also produced and distributed *Der Weg zum Sieg*, sub-titled Information Service of the KPD, and signed apparently by the CC of the KPD. It presented a broad brush ultra-optimistic approach: join anti-fascist revolutionary struggle, and showed little recognition of how badly the German working class had been defeated.[26]

By June 1941, Baum and others from his group such as Marianne Baum had become forced labourers at the electric motor works division of Siemens, *Etno-Werke*, where there were around 500 Jewish forced labourers. In early 1941, 30,000 Jews were conscripted as forced labourers, about 20% of the remaining Jews in Germany. Then all Jews aged 15-65 were forced into labour, an additional 73,000 for war related industries. Baum became the forced labourers' representative, campaigning, remarkably, for improvements in working conditions and the minimum wage. They collaborated with Dutch and French slave labourers in a resistance cell of about fifteen, which aimed to commit sabotage.[27]

In April 1942, ten people carried out mass graffiting, painting "No to Hitler's suicidal policies" on many walls. Then in May 1942, Baum and a few others, attempted to expropriate rich Jewish families by confiscating their possessions in order to fund the struggle. They produced a new pamphlet "Organise the Mass Revolutionary Struggle against fascism and imperialist war" arguing for the transition from imperialist to civil war. And again, in May 1942 they wrote and sent an open letter to the party calling for increased activity and to prepare for Hitler's defeat in the summer, one of the few documents to survive.[28] Baum, it has been suggested, was too influenced by the line of the Comintern and too much of an optimist, expecting Germany to soon be defeated.

These groups were tiny and fluid. Baum and his group began collaborating with the

---

24 Hoss,Christiane and Schönfeld, Martin, "Plaques in Berlin. Places of memory of the persecuted of National Socialism" *The Active Museum of Fascism and Resistance in Berlin*, Vol 9
25 Brothers, *Berlin Ghetto*
26 John Cox, 2009, *Circle of Resistance: Jewish, leftist and youth dissidence in Nazi Germany* , Frankfurt: Peter Lang,
27 Brothers, *Berlin Ghetto*
28 Ibid.

Joachim Group, organised by Heinz Joachim, notable because its handful of members were equally women and men. They also worked with the Franke-Steinbrink group, a small KPD band, led by Joachim Franke (KPD until 1928) and Werner Steinbrink (KJVD), who was a chemical technician.

One of the best known acts of resistance employing violent means, other than the actual attempts to kill Hitler, was made possible by Steinbrink. In mid-May 1942, he made the detonating material for the arson attack on the anti-Soviet and anti-Semitic propaganda exhibition "The Soviet Paradise" in Berlin's *Lustgarten* on May 18, 1942. Eleven members, including Hildegard Jadamowitz and Marianne Baum invaded the exhibition and set fire to it at different points. The attack was only partially successful. They were arrested a few days later, and sentenced to death.

Hildegard Jadamowitz

Let us also pause to recognise one of the leading women in the workers' resistance. Hildegard Jadamowitz joined the Communist Youth League in 1931 as a fifteen-year-old, from 1933 she was a factory worker and saleswoman and a member of the KPD operating cell in the Lorenz AG in Tempelhof. She leafleted on behalf of the Joachim Franke group and was in touch with other resistance groups. On May 22, 1942, she was arrested by the Gestapo and on July 16, sentenced to death by decapitation.

Foreign Workers and Soviet POWs

While these groups are not German workers, they became a part of the German industrial workforce and deserve a mention. The German war economy depended increasingly on slave/camp labour or 'alien labour', especially in armaments and defence, which made sabotage more possible. At the Mittelbau-Dora camp where parts for the V2 were manufactured, prisoners assembled the parts badly and worked as slowly as possible.[29] Though documentation is thin on the ground, 'alien workers', whether through exhaustion or resistance, attempted go-slows and sabotage, for which, if suspected, they would receive the severest of punishments.[30]

In the camps, Russian POWs, altogether about 5.7 million (of whom 3.3 m had 'died' by the end of the war) were the particular target of the Nazis. Remarkably, they organised resistance groups in the camps, made contact with German antifascists, made easier as

29 http://drapeau-rouge.tumblr.com/post/159764462894/the-hidden-war-working-class-resistance
30 Peukert, *Inside Nazi Germany*

54

they were used as forced labour on the land and in factories and, when 'at work', committed acts of sabotage, distributed leaflets and prepared for armed struggle.[31]

In the last months of the war, in Cologne, there were quasi-partisan battles in autumn 1944 when escaped POWs, foreign workers, German anti-fascists and the young Edelweiss pirates carried out surprise attacks on military supply sites and full scale assaults on Gestapo officials.[32] Gestapo records from 1943 reveal a surprising number of arrests for contact with POWs, but by far the largest number of arrests were for Soviet forced labourers going on strike.

Opposition within the army: desertion as a form of resistance

I suspect desertion was far more common than is appreciated. The precise numbers are unknown. There were between 300,000 and 500,000 deserters altogether by the end of 1944 out of a total of about 12 million conscripts, figures which some historians consider too high.[33] Moreover, from mid-1944, when desertion almost certainly rose, the collection of statistics in the *Wehrmacht* began to break down. And for our purposes, deserters who were 'merely' attempting to avoid fighting, and quite possibly dying, for the Nazis need to be distinguished from those who were 'active deserters'.

The 999 Division included 'active deserters'. From 2nd October 1942, men who had previously been considered "unworthy of the army" or "war criminals" or who had committed sabotage or tried to desert were recruited for service in the *Wehrmacht* in the *Strafdivision* 999 (Punishment Division 999).[34] This was made up of about one third politically convicted, one third other persecuted persons, including minor criminals and about one-third Nazis who were of course the guards, commanders and the like. Between September 1942 and September 1944, about 28,000 were drafted. The "political" cover the entire spectrum of German resistance: anarchists who fought in the Spanish Civil War with the International Brigades, as ever the most hated of all the groups, along with Communists, Social Democrats and other socialists. Jehovah's Witnesses were also included. These unwilling conscripts were sent into action in Tunisia, Greece and on the Eastern Front.

A recent German radio programme contained interviews with surviving veterans of *Strafdivision 999*.[35] About a third were Communists, for example, Kurt Neukircher, who had distributed anti-Nazi leaflets in the Zwickau region. Neukircher survived because he

31 Wachsmann, *History of the Nazi Concentration Camps*
32 Peukert, *Inside Nazi Germany*
33 Willner in Mannfred Messerschmidt, 1991,*Germany and the Second World War*, München: Deutsche Verlags-Anstalt. Messerschmidt was the long-term research director at the Military History Research Office
34 http://www.deutschlandfunk.de/die-soldaten-mit-dem-blauen-schein-txt-dokument.media.306728e1caa1cac7c486a0f34be82afa.txt. My thanks to Steve Cushion for his help with this section.
35 Christian Blees, *Die Soldaten mit dem blauen Schein - "Wehrunwürdige" in der Strafdivision 999*, Deutschlandfunk, 26.May.2009, 19.15 – 20.00

deserted into English captivity in Tunisia, and later bore witness to what had happened. He describes how two bible students had been shot for refusing to wear a uniform or carry a weapon.

Another former political prisoner, Erwin Schulz told the interviewer: "Yes, yes, tomorrow is the First of May, we're not going to become captives just yet - we want to see the May 1st as free people between the front-lines." And then, the next day, they headed on to the Allied lines where they were captured by Moroccans.

The unit was saved from being sent in its entirety to Russia for fear that the men would just melt away into the Soviet army. Some deserters had obtained a loudspeaker from the Red Army and used it to publicise their grievances. "And indeed, the very next day four 999ers disarmed their sergeant and deserted over the ice to the Russians. Of course, all the alarm bells rang out. The commanders then decided to disarm all the political people in this battalion immediately".

After this event, all of the 999 battalions stationed on the Eastern Front, were disarmed, imprisoned and then sent back to Germany where they were court martialed. However, it could not be proved that more than a few of the more than 400 soldiers from the punishment battalion were actually involved in the desertions. As a result, the army command assembled all the politicals in a newly formed battalion and dispatched them to a front-line mission in Greece. Once there, the 999s immediately began to organise political resistance on the ground. Many deserted to the Greek partisans.

One 999 veteran, Hans-Peter Klausch stated that wherever the opponents of Hitler's Germany came into contact with the 999s, they became acquainted with the other Germany: the Germany of resistance. And this often left a positive impression on the occupied peoples and Allied armies. In Greece, for instance, the graves of the 999s who were executed were decorated with flowers and wreaths by the Greek people. And when it came to the victory parades everywhere in the Greek cities after the departure of the Germans in November '44, there were always 999s in German uniform involved in these demonstrations. As a result of their resistance, the German reputation stood better than it would have been without their fight.

One of the many intriguing aspects of this story is how far the Communists in the 999 brigade, even though holding internationalist principles, saw themselves as the "good" Germans against the "criminals": the torturers who had tyrannised and therefore did not represent the true Germany.

Joining the other side

I want to end by mentioning the very few members of the armed forces who went over to "the other side". Though literature on this is scarce and though estimated numbers vary, what emerges is the breadth of reasons given by members of the armed forces who joined the other side and survived.[36]

Peter Schilling had volunteered for the artillery but observing what the Germans were doing to the enemy and influenced by a brush with Marxism, decided to escape and got into Switzerland. Ludwig Baumann, a bricklayer from Hamburg, was conscripted and, transferred to France, became friends with some French dockers and defected because he did not want to be part of this "murdering war", but not before he had stolen some weapons. He was then helped by French resistance fighters and distributed illegal papers to German troops. Helmut Kober, whose parents were Social Democrats, was drafted, could not bear what he saw and when his unit was sent to Upper Silesia, deserted to the Red Army.

A handful of other German soldiers found their way to the USSR, to be distinguished from the Communist cadre who had fled to the USSR.[37] Heinz Kessler, who had been drafted into the *Wehrmacht* in 1940, defected to the Red Army in 1941 when on a spying mission and then joined the Red Army: it seems his role was to "educate" prisoners of war. In 1943, he was involved in founding the National Committee for a Free Germany (*Nationalkomitee Freies Deutschland*, or NKFD).

Franz Gold seems to have been the one person who may have used arms on behalf of the Red Army. After erratic membership of the KPD, he was drafted into the *Wehrmacht* in September 1940. In September 1941, he joined the Red Army as a private and then worked as a propagandist in German POW camps. He was trained as a partisan and participated in August / September 1944 in the Slovak uprising as commander of a partisan unit, reaching Moravia and Bohemia.[38]

Rudolph Jacobs, who was drafted in 1939 and rose to the rank of captain, joined the Italian Garibaldi partisans, and in 1944 was killed. Heinz Riedt was also able to escape the *Wehrmacht*, moved to Padua and in 1943, joined the *Giustizia e Libertà* partisan group.

The National Committee for a Free Germany, was initiated by the Soviet leadership in July 1943 to persuade German POWs of the correctness of the democratic anti-Nazi case. The NKFD focused on propaganda: they translated propaganda material into German, produced their own newspaper and radio station, sent leaflets to German soldiers at the front and POWs in the Soviet camps. They prepared broadcasts directed at the POWs, and on occasion interrogated captured German officers. They appealed to the German soldiers to desert. Some NKFD members were attached to front line Soviet units to interrogate

---

36 Peterson, Lars, 2013, *Hitlers Deserters,* Stroud: Fonthill.
37 Veyrier, Marcel, 1970, *La Wehrmacht Rouge, Moscou 1943-1945,* Paris: Julliard.
38 https://de.wikipedia.org/wiki/Franz_Gold

German POWs and for propaganda purposes.[39]

The NKFD used conservative symbols and ideology. For example, the old flag colours of Imperial Germany were used instead of the Weimar flag. The stated goal of the NKFD organisation was for the opening of peace negotiations and the deposing and punishment of the Nazi leadership. The NKFD presented their case in terms of German civilians and soldiers placing the interests of the German nation above those of their Nazi leaders. No specific appeal was made to the German working class to rise up.[40]

Its president was the exiled Erich Weinert; the leadership included 28 *Wehrmacht* POWs and 10 exiled communists. These included Wilhelm Pieck (who in 1938 had become the General Secretary of the Communist International in Moscow and was to be the first President of East Germany) and Walter Ulbricht, who lived in the Soviet Union from 1937 to 1945. After the defeat of the German army at Stalingrad, they recruited about 20 German officers, including the German commander Von Paulus who saw Hitler as leading Germany to defeat and about 350 POWs.[41]

Conclusion

Why was resistance not more extensive or more radical? Such was the terror launched against the left, in particular the Communists, that just surviving and keeping their organisation in existence underground became the priority of the resistance groups. Distributing illegal leaflets, circulating information, maintaining contacts and supporting the persecuted and their families took much solidarity and courage but hardly threatened the Nazi regime.

The extent to which the resistance, even from within the workers' movement saw itself as opposing Germany as a capitalist system or wanted Germany to lose the war is impossible to estimate. We have virtually none of the illegal publications they distributed nor many other documents. Very few survived to tell their stories and even those who did often chose not to speak. There were also the inevitable differences within the Left as to how far the struggle should have had as its goal revolutionary upheaval or whether overthrowing Nazism was the only pragmatic choice. What comes across is that much of the resistance saw the Nazis as the bad Germans and that they were the good Germans. Yet some of the groups associated with the KPD that were more rooted in the working class movement emphasised, along with calls to join the resistance, the importance of issues relating to class, such as wages, the cost of living etc.

This article has deliberately not looked at parts of the resistance which are better known. The resistance from within the German working class movement is all but unknown,

39 Veyrier, *La Wehrmacht Rouge*, pp 48-51, 131
40 *Ibid.* pp. 90, 91, 116/17
41 *Ibid.* p.116

certainly in Britain, but also, I suggest, generally, in Germany. The Nazis murdered many of these brave men and women. It is up to us now to stand in our comrades shoes and carry on their struggle against the growing threat of racism and Nazism.

Bibliography

A note: as anybody familiar with the literature on this topic knows, there are massive methodological issues about ascertaining the extent, beliefs and effectiveness of groups rooted in the working class resistance, which there is just no space to explore. However, a few brief pointers: the Nazis destroyed much documentation, the allies' bombing destroyed other documentation, the "official" judicial bits of the Nazi state tend to use vague words like 'traitors' about the people they sentence, the post- war Restitution Courts were far from even-handed and anyway dead comrades couldn't claim, the resistance, of course didn't keep minutes and much of the resistance didn't live to tell their stories. Increasingly there is an attempt, and with much difficulty, to construct stories locally but then, as the researchers themselves state (at length), this is still a micro, not a macro, view and may well not be typical.

Brothers, Eric, *Berlin Ghetto. Herbert Baum and the Anti-Nazi Resistance*, The History Press, 2012

Cox, John: *Circle of Resistance: Jewish, leftist and youth dissidence in Nazi Germany*, Peter Lang, 2009

Hoss, Christiane, Martin Schönfeld: *Plaques in Berlin. Places of memory of the persecuted of National Socialism in* The Active Museum of Fascism and Resistance in Berlin eV Vol 9

Mason, Tim, 'The Containment of the Working Class in Nazi Germany', in *Nazism, Fascism and the Working Class*, Cambridge, 1995.

Merson, Allan, *Communist Resistance in Nazi Germany*, Lawrence and Wishart , 1985

Peterson, Lars, *Hitler's Deserters*, Fonthill Media, 2013

Peukert, Detlev, *Inside Nazi Germany*, GB, B.T.Batesford Ltd, 1987

Rosenstock, Werner, "The Jewish Youth Movement" in Leo Baeck, *Institute Year Book* 19, 1974

Veyrier, Marcel, *La Wehrmacht Rouge, Moscou 1943-45*, Format books, 1970.

Wachsmann, Nikolaus, *A History of the Nazi Concentration Camps*, 2015, Little, Brown, London

Willner in Messerschmidt, Mannfred, *Germany and the Second World War*, Deutsche Verlags-Anstalt, 1991

Walter Pätzold - German Soldier and Italian Partisan

from the testimony of *Irene Recksiek*, translated by *Irena Fick.*[1]

This photograph tells an intriguing story of resistance in troubled times. It is on an ID card and shows a man in German army uniform. However, closer inspection of the top right-hand corner shows the stamp of the *Brigate d'Assalto Garibaldi*, the communist section of the Italian anti-fascist partisans. The *Istituto piemontese per la storia della Resistenza e della società contemporanea* in Turin holds an index card for the Partisan Walter Pätzold, the man in the photo.

Walter Pätzold

The Garibaldi Brigades were partisan units organized by the Italian Communist Party and fighting as part of the Italian resistance during the Second World War. Composed mostly of communists, they were the largest of the partisan groups organised under the umbrella *Comitato di Liberazione Nazionale* (Committee of National Liberation, or CLN) and suffered the greatest total losses during the partisan war. These brigades were distinguished by the red scarves worn around their necks.

Historical background: In July 1943, following a vote of the Fascist Grand Council (*Gran Consiglio del Fascismo*), the main body of Fascist government in Italy, Mussolini was deposed by the King, arrested and held prisoner. From this time onwards, Italy was engaged in negotiations with the allied forces until the beginning of September 1943. These negotiations culminated in the signing of an armistice agreement and a ceasefire was announced shortly thereafter. The German army immediately invaded and occupied the North of Italy, provoking a massive resistance movement that had to fight both the German occupying forces and the Italian fascists still loyal to Mussolini. It thus became both a war against German occupation and a civil war.[2] The *Piemonte* region was a stronghold of the partisan movement, with many thousands of combatants by mid-April 1945, when the increasingly militant activities of the partisans spilled over into a general strike and insurrection.[3]

---

1 We are most grateful for the testimony written by Irene Recksiek about her father, Walter Pätzold. It was translated by Irena Fick. Without their help we would not have known about this fascinating history.
2 Tom Behan, *The Italian Resistance: Fascists, Guerrillas and the Allies*, London: Pluto Press (2009); Claudio Pavone, *A Civil War: A History of the Italian Resistance*, London: Verso (2014)
3 We only have rough estimates of the number of resistance fighters in regional partisan brigades and total number of fighters and these figures vary enormously. See Battaglia, Roberto and Garritano, Giuseppe, *Der Italienische Widerstandskampf*, 1943 bis 1945, Berlin: Deutscher Militärverlag, p.158

The partisan liberation of each city began in Bologna. By 21st April 1945, the town was free of German occupying troops. Reggio Emilia was freed on 24th April. Milan followed on 25th April 1945. On this date, the CLN for Northern Italy called for a national uprising, which followed a general strike that commenced on 18th April 1945. Turin and Bergamo were also liberated by 28th April 1945.

Günther Meinhold, the commander of German troops in Genoa, deliberately disobeyed Hitler's orders not to surrender on any account. He held negotiations with the regional CLN and together with partisan leaders, signed the armistice agreement on 25th April 1945. He and the soldiers under his command were captured on 26th and 27th April 1945. This was a unique response from a German city commandant in Italy. However, in their effort to crush the partisan movement, the Germans were responsible for countless massacres from September 1943, even during their retreat. Their victims were often innocent civilians, including many children.

So, where does Walter Pätzold fit into this? His daughter, Irene Recksiek, has researched Walter Pätzold's life and during her research, found the photo and index card proving that her father was an active member of the Italian partisans. She also tells us that Walter Pätzold was born in 1906 in Silesia, a province in the East of the former German Empire. As a young man he had been politically active, first in the Social Democratic Party and then later with the Communists.

Walter Pätzold was arrested, along with thousands of other socialists, communists and trade unionists on 4th March 1933, the day before the last multi-party elections, although the campaign had already been the subject of considerable Nazi brutality against representatives of the other parties and could not be considered "free".

He was first taken to the prison in Hirschberg (today Jelena Góra), later to a prison in the then capital of Silesia, Breslau (today Wrocław). He was subsequently held, in the form of internment without trial known as "protective custody", at the KZ Esterwegen concentration camp situated in the northern region of the former German Empire from 10th August 1933 until the so-called "Christmas Amnesty" at the end of 1933. Little is known of his life in the time before the war, when he lived with his parents, working in their grocery shop. The country changed dramatically during his imprisonment of almost a year. Civil liberties were abolished and apart from the National Socialist Party, all other parties and unions were banned. Oppositional political activities were only possible if done illegally.

The Second World War began in September 1939 and Walter Patzöld was conscripted into the *Wehrmacht* in February 1940. He was initially attached to a construction regiment, then after November 1940 to the *Munitions-Verwaltungs-Kompanie 577* (Ordinance Maintenance Company 577). We do not know where this unit spent most of the war, but it was eventually based in Villastellone near Turin in Northern Italy. The local chronicles of Villastellone (by Antonio Alasia) tell us of the "Deployment of around 80 members of the *Wehrmacht* after June 1944". The soldiers built and managed a large ammunition depot, the largest in west Piedmont, in a villa surrounded by parkland, in the centre of the village.

Irene Recksiek has tried to find contemporary witnesses. One of these had a father who himself was a partisan. Walter Pätzold and his family visited Italy in the 1950s. As a child, this witness had observed a meeting of his father with Walter Pätzold. He said he could see how Walter Pätzold was warmly welcomed as an old and trusted friend, as they knew each other from their days as partisans.

Irene Recksiek tells us: *"My father definitely didn't desert the army. He was still part of his company until the end of the war. I couldn't find out what my father did as a partisan. There are obviously no written records. It would also have been far too dangerous, as supporting the partisans was something that could never have been made public. In that respect, we can only speculate about what he might have done. It is possible that he smuggled ammunition from the depot to the partisans. A witness reported that the ammunition held at the depot was booby-trapped and an explosion anywhere in the vicinity would have caused the whole of the depot to explode, destroying a large part of Villastellone itself. It is believed in Villastellone that Walter Pätzold disconnected the fuses, thereby saving the town from destruction.*

My father always used to talk about how he had managed to prevent the deliberate detonation of an ammunition transportation by retreating German soldiers during the final days of the war."

It may come as a surprise that there is a partisan ID card for Walter Pätzold. To be caught with such a document during the war would have meant certain death. If you take a closer look at the document, you can see that his membership of the partisan movement was not issued until after the war was over, so that Walter Pätzold could openly proclaim his allegiance to the *Brigate d'Assalto Garibaldi*. No matter, we can be glad that it has given us the opportunity to recover the history of a courageous man.

Irene Recksiek and her sister were born in Italy and grew up in the Federal Republic of Germany. They had a very politically active father, who was always afraid that the Nazis could regain power. This is explained by his biography. After the war, he never openly talked about his partisan activities. Most Germans would not have understood and would have criticised his involvement, but he was celebrated for this in Italy.

Major Karl Plagge and Sergeant Anton Schmid [1]

Steve Cushion

Three days after the German invasion of the USSR, German tanks reached the Lithuanian city of Vilnius, which only a year previously had been occupied by Russian troops. A considerable proportion of the Lithuanian population welcomed the Germans in the mistaken expectation that they would restore national independence. With the invading German troops came *Einsatzgruppe A* (Special Forces A) and, before they left town at the end of July 1941, they had, together with local auxiliary forces, murdered 5,000 Jews. Even before German troops arrived Lithuanian anti-communists, who had fought against the Russian occupation, committed atrocities against Jews and communists. Of particular danger were the so-called "snatchers", Lithuanian anti-semites who would grab Jews off the street at random and murder them.

The brutality of local anti-semites even surprised the SS. In Kaunas during the night of 25-26th June 1941 Lithuanian anti-communists started a pogrom without prior German orders during which 1,500 Jews, including women and children, were massacred, several synagogues destroyed, and a Jewish district of 60 houses burnt down. In the following nights another 2,300 Jews were killed. The first organized mass executions took place in Ponary near Vilnius, where 40,000 Jews were shot and by December 1941, 137, 346 Jews had been murdered. Ghettos were erected in major Lithuanian cities. In Vilnius two ghettos were created, one for Jews able to work and another for those Jews unable to work, who would be systematically killed. By December 1941 about 12,000 "Work Jews" remained in the ghetto legally in addition to around 8,000 illegal Jews in hiding places.

On 23rd January 1942 various resistance groups in Vilnius united to form the *Fareinikte Partisaner Organiszje* (FPO - United Partisan Organization). Three hundred fighters, including many women, formed two battalions. The first leader of the FPO was Jizchak Wittenberg, a life-long communist, but whose non-sectarian approach allowed him to forge a unified resistance movement comprised of Communists, Bundists, and Zionists. Immediately following the German occupation he went underground, but on 16 July 1943 the Gestapo threatened to bomb the ghetto if the Jewish council did not extradite Wittenberg. He surrendered voluntarily and was shot the same day. He was succeeded by Abba Kovner, a member of *Haschomer Hazair*, a left-wing Zionist organization. When the Ghetto of Vilnius was liquidated on 23 September 1943, a few partisans, among them Kovner, succeeded in escaping into the woods. About 3,000 "Work Jews" remained in the ghetto but the majority of the remaining ghetto inmates were sent to the Sobibor extermination camp. On 3 July 1944, 10 days before the Red Army liberated Vilnius, most of the remaining "work Jews" were murdered in Ponary. Of the 57,000 Jews of Vilnius,

---

1 For a fuller account see: Schoeps, Karl-Heinz, "Holocaust and Resistance in Vilnius: Rescuers in *"Wehrmacht"* Uniforms", *German Studies Review*, Vol. 31, No. 3 (Oct., 2008), pp. 489-512

only two or three thousand survived.

Major Karl Plagge came to Vilnius in early July 1941, where he became commander of *Heereskraftfahrpark 562* (HKP - Army Vehicle Maintenance Unit). He remained in Vilnius until the army left in July 1944. Plagge not only employed Jewish mechanics in his workshop but also Jews without any qualifications in order to save them from the *Einsatzkommandos*. He had several confrontations with Nazi officials to protect his Jewish employees. He succeeded in freeing some of them from Lukiskis prison, thus saving them from execution in Ponary. In 1942 more foreign workers were wanted for the home industry in Germany and Plagge's Jewish workers were threatened with deportation. When Plagge learned that some of his workers were being loaded on a train, he and a group of *Wehrmacht* soldiers under his command went to the station in order to try to free them, but to

Major Karl Plagge

no avail. When the Vilnius Ghetto was dissolved in September 1943, Plagge arranged for a separate camp to be established for his workshop. It accommodated between 1,000 and 1,500 Jewish men and their immediate families.

In the summer of 1944, Major Plagge returned to Germany with the retreating *Wehrmacht* and the SS set about butchering the camp's inmates. About 75 finally managed to escape, while another 200 managed to hide and survive the war. Plagge said in 1957 "*if on earth there should only be 'scourges and victims,' then it is an obligation to stand, not on the side of the castigator, but to espouse the cause of the victim*".[2]

But if Karl Plagge sought to protect Jewish people from the Nazis, Sergeant Anton Schmid went further and took an active part in the Jewish resistance. A radio repair engineer from Vienna, he helped some Jewish friends escape to Czechoslovakia following the German annexation of Austria. He was briefly arrested when he slapped a Nazi who had broken the window of a Jewish baker. He was conscripted into the *Wehrmacht* on the outbreak of war and, like Plagge, found himself managing a carpentry workshop in Vilnius employing about 100 "Work Jews" who he sought to protect.

He managed to contact Jewish resistance groups in the ghetto and became friends with Jewish resistance leaders such as Mordecai Tennenbaum and Abba Kovner; he was made

2 Michael Good, *The Search for Major Plagge: The Nazi Who Saved Jews* (New York: Fordham University Press, 2005, p.223. Michael Good the son of Pearl Good, a survivor of the Vilnius Ghetto and Plagge's camp.

an honorary member of *Haschomer Hazair*. He procured weapons for the resistance and transported Jewish partisans in his *Wehrmacht* trucks to the ghettos of Bialystock and Warsaw. His apartment in Vilnius was a safe haven for Jewish partisans where they could rest and plot their activities with advice from Schmid. In February 1942, he was arrested, tried by a German military court, sentenced to death, and executed on 13 April 1942.

After her husband's death, neighbours reviled Frau Schmid as the wife of a traitor and attempted to drive her from the neighbourhood by smashing her windows. In 1965 Simon Wiesenthal arranged for her to visit to her husband's grave in Vilnius, where the inscription reads: "*Here Rests A Man Who Thought It Was More Important To Help His Fellow Men Than To Live*".

Sergeant Anton Schmid

German and Italian Volunteers in the French Resistance

Steve Cushion

There was a surprising number of "foreign" volunteers in the French Resistance, a fact barely recognised today as the history of the Resistance has been nationalised and has become the founding myth of the French Republic, rather as the myths of Dunkirk and the Blitz are used in Britain. Probably the most important section were the exiled Spanish "Guerrrilleros" who operated in the South West and who led the battle for the liberation of Toulouse. But theirs is a story of its own for another day; this article will look at the German and Italian fighters as they were directly involved in traitorous activities against troops of their home nations. But nevertheless their story starts in Spain where there were somewhere in the region of 8,000 German, Austrian and Italian volunteers in the International Brigades and, of course, these volunteers were engaged in fighting against the armies of the lands of their birth even then. The Battle of Guadalajara, March 1937, is probably most famous. The whole Italian expeditionary corps of 35,000 soldiers, with 80 tanks and 200 field guns, supported by German aircraft, tried to break through to Madrid and they were defeated by Spanish Republican troops with the Italian-speaking Garibaldi and German-speaking Thälmann Battalions at the front.

When the Spanish Republic took the ill-advised decision to disband the International Brigade in October 1938, the Italian, German and Austrian volunteers had nowhere to return to and most ended up as refugees in France, where the majority were interned in concentration camps, where they were kept in vile conditions. They were joined in the camps by many other anti-fascist German refugees who were rounded up as "undesirable aliens" at the outbreak of the Second Word War, although a number did manage to join the French Foreign Legion. The mobilisation of the French army left many areas short of labour and the government set up *Compagnies de Travailleurs Étrangers* (CTE - Companies of Foreign Workers) to organise some of the inmates of the camps into companies of 250 men to replace mobilised French labour in the defence industries, agriculture and forestry. Thus, when the French Army collapsed in 1940 in the face of the German invasion, many of these political prisoners were outside the camps and in a condition of partial freedom.[1]

The big difference between the German and Italian political refugees in France was the existence of a large Italian immigration already present in the country, probably a million and a half, most of whom were present as "economic migrants", but for a significant number, a good part of their reason for emigrating was their hatred of Fascism. This Italian / French population was concentrated in the mining regions of the Pas-de-Calais and Lorraine as well as the rural South West, particularly the Lot-et-Garonne. Italian Fascism

---

1 Peschanski, Denis, 2000, *Les camps français d'internement (1938-1946)*, Doctorat d'Etat: Université Panthéon-Sorbonne

had been active in France from long before the war, much of the French bourgeoisie had great sympathy for Mussolini, while there was active collaboration between the French and Italian extreme right. In June 1937, the French right-wing terrorist organisation, "La Cagoule", murdered the Italian social-democrat Carlo Rosselli on the instructions of the Italian Foreign Ministry.[2]

Eusebio Ferrari

In the mining regions, the employers were strongly pro-fascist and the Italian mining families suffered considerable xenophobic discrimination. By 1941, there was a second generation of this Italian immigration, often French citizens by birth but, remembering the only party that had defended their parents, were extremely loyal to the Communist Party. The North-East corner of France, the Forbidden Zone, was cut off from the rest of the country and the local communists operated independently of Paris, so while the Paris leadership of the PCF was still observing the terms of the Hitler-Stalin pact, they were preparing for resistance in the Pas-de-Calais. In May 1941, there was a week-long strike involving 100,000 miners, a strike in which the Italian miners played a prominent role. The miners won their demands, but many of the strike-leaders had to go underground to escape the resulting repression. Living in the relative security provided by the traditional solidarity of mining communities, an armed resistance developed in the region, considerably in advance of the rest of the country.[3] One of the most successful of these groups was led by a young Italian electrician, Eusebio Ferrari, who organised a series of increasingly audacious [or reckless, depending on your point of view] sabotage attacks, including several train derailments, and one of the first direct attacks on German soldiers. He was finally cornered by the French police and shot dead in February 1942. His group was composed of young Italian, French and Polish workers, but also one young German exile, Paul Hanke.[4]

Given the large scale immigration into France following the First World War, the CGTU trade union federation, under PCF leadership, had set up *Main-d'œuvre immigrée* (MOI - Immigrant Labour) to organise these migrant workers. It was divided into language sections, principally Polish, Italian, Yiddish and Spanish. These sections became the basis

2 Pugliese, Stanislao G., 1997, "Death in Exile: The Assassination of Carlo Rosselli", *Journal of Contemporary History*, Sage Publications, Ltd. vol.32 no.3, pp.305-319
3 Dejonghe, Étienne, 1986 "Les communistes dans le Nord/Pas-de-Calais de juin 1940 à la veille de la grève des mineurs" *Revue du Nord*, tome 68, n°270, Juillet-septembre, pp. 685-720.
4 Pierrart, André & Rousseau, Michel, 1980, *Eusébio Ferrari* Paris: Editions Syros.

for the organisation for resistance by foreign workers. The French Communist Party set up the *Francs-tireurs et partisans* (FTP) at the end of 1941, to act as an armed resistance organisation, the different groups of the MOI organised armed groups, FTP-MOI, based loosely on the different language sections. Although in theory subject to the same military command as the FTP, difficulties in communication due to language differences and the demands of a clandestine existence, as well as each national grouping also having a political agenda linked to their countries of origin, meant that these groups operated with a high degree of independence.

The largest of these was the "35th Brigade" of the FTP-MOI, operating around Toulouse, led by a Pole, Mendel Langer, with, as political commissar, one of the few women who rose to military leadership in the resistance, Catherine Varlin, a French communist born in Odessa of Jewish Romanian heritage. She eventually became the commander of the FTP in the Meuse region of Lorraine, commanding a unit composed of 289 escaped Russian prisoners of war along with 34 Yugoslavs, 45 Poles and 14 French.[5] Let us not forget that Romania was part of the Axis, so she also counts as a traitor. The FTP-MOI of the Toulouse area carried out multiple urban guerrilla actions: destruction of communication axes like the railways or the Midi Canal, sabotage of electricity pylons, individual as well as assassination attempts against German soldiers in cinemas and restaurants. Mendel Langer was captured in February 1943 and at his trial, the prosecutor, Pierre Lespinasse said "*vous êtes juif, étranger et communiste... Voilà trois raisons pour que vous soyez exécuté*".[6] He was guillotined in July 1943, but the prosecutor was gunned down by Langer's comrades in the following October. The Vichy government set up special anti-terrorist courts in 1941, but the FTP-MOI developed the tactic of shooting the magistrates who condemned their comrades to death, which had the effect of making it much more difficult to find lawyers willing to serve on these *sections spéciales*.

The North of the area covered by the 35th brigade, the Lot-et-Garonne, was an area with a long tradition of Italian immigration, mainly farmers and agricultural labourers, who had maintained their traditional loyalty to the Italian communist party. The PCI could count on the loyalty of around 150 families in the area round the departmental capital Agen, providing a solid basis for the Italian section of the FTP-MOI. Led by Fiore Lorenzi, his son Enzo and Maria Lesizza, not only did they provide a significant number of fighters, they were also able to shelter many resistance fighters on the run in farms in the region. Their first loyalty was to the PCI rather than the PCF and retained a certain independence. Thus, against PCF advice, they assassinated Cardinal Torricelli, who organised propaganda in favour of Fascist Italy in Agen, and when the Italian partisan movement really got going in 1943, a considerable number of Italian resistance fighters crossed the

5 Collin, Claude, 1994, "Étrangers Et Nos Frères Pourtant: Contribution à L'histoire Des Francs-Tireurs Et Partisans de la Main-D'œuvre Immigrée", *Guerres Mondiales et Conflits Contemporains*, no. 174, pp. 161–177.
6 "You are a Jew, a foreigner and a communist, three reasons for you to be executed"

Alps to join the fight in Italy. It is clear that there were different motivations within the Italian sections of the FTP-MOI and, while the more established immigrants and especially their children, now French citizens, were much more likely to see themselves a part of a specifically French resistance, the more recent immigrants and political refugees, saw the fighting in France as a stage on the road back to fighting their home-grown fascism back in Italy.

There was a particularly important FTP-MOI movement based in Lyon and Grenoble, *Compagnie Carmagnole-Liberté*. This was initially mainly composed of Yiddish-speaking immigrant workers from Central Europe, with the Italians joining later. This was partly because repression hit the Jewish immigrants much earlier and force of circumstances increased the need for militants to go underground. The initial role of the more settled Italian community in the region was to provide support for these clandestine fighters: safe houses, provisions, armaments etc. This was essential to the success of the urban guerrillas and, in many ways, more dangerous as they were sitting-ducks for the forces of repression.

South East France was occupied by the Italian Army after 1942 and the Italian section of the MOI, led by Teresa Noce, an exiled communist textile worker and trade unionist, conducted propaganda amongst the occupation forces, publishing a duplicated sheet "*Parola del Soldato*" and setting up *Comité d'action du peuple italien* (Italian People's Action Committee). The Italian community in Grenoble was particularly successful in fraternising with Italian conscript soldiers and passing propaganda. An old communist from 1923, Joseph Buffa, managed to trade food for hand grenades and a rifle when he discovered that two soldiers in the local garrison were relatives of his wife. They had a modest success in encouraging desertions before 1943, but this activity really paid off when Mussolini was deposed in 1943 and the new Italian government changed sides. The German Army started to round up Italian soldiers and the MOI was able to help several thousand of them to desert and either go underground in France or return to Italy. There was fighting that left 100 dead when German soldiers disarmed the garrison in Grenoble.[7]

Many of those Italian activists wishing to return to fight in Italy gathered in Marseilles, from where they sought secret passages over the Alps. Meanwhile, they took an active part in the resistance in the Alp-Maritimes region. The large Italian community based round the bauxite mines in Brignoles was not only the centre of recruitment for the armed struggle;it was the scene of extended strike action in January-March 1942. The Italian IV Army, the main force occupying South East France collapsed in July-September 1943, soldiers committees were set up and thousands deserted, while several dozen joined the FTP. In the confusion, the leading Italian activists crossed back into Italy where there they put their

---

7 Collin, Claude, 2005, "Les Italiens dans la M.O.I et les FTP-MOI à Lyon et Grenoble." *Guerres Mondiales Et Conflits Contemporains*, no. 218, pp. 67–83.

experience to use and became leading partisan militants.[8] On a more domestic note, a number of Italian soldiers used the collapse of the Italian forces of occupation to marry their local girlfriends and lose themselves in the local population.[9]

If the destabilisation efforts amongst the Italian soldiers had proved relatively successful, propaganda amongst soldiers in the *Wehrmacht* was to prove more difficult and dangerous. There was not the same German-speaking community established in France and the 50,000 refugees who arrived in the 1930s were treated from the beginning as "undesirable aliens". Of these maybe 4,500 were communists and 3,500 social-democrats. Many writers create what, in my view, is a false distinction between political refugees and Jewish refugees. Many of the politicals were of Jewish heritage, while many of the Jews were politicised by their experiences of repression and exile. As part of the Armistice agreement, the Vichy government agreed to hand over all German residents to the Nazis and in October 1940, Pétain ordered the rounding up of the Jews. In passing, let us note that news of the death camps reached Paris in May 1942 and was publicised in clandestine resistance newspapers urging Jewish people to escape at all cost. So after this date, the French police who continued their arrests of Jews knew exactly what fate was in store for them. So the situation of the German-speaking resistance was much more precarious than the Italian experience. Nevertheless, considerable effort was put into propaganda amongst German soldiers.

There were two main approaches, the communist *Travail Allemand* or TA, distributed a paper *Soldat im Westen*, which took a fairly "patriotic" line, "we are the good Germans, the Nazis are the traitors", while the Trotskyists had *Arbeiter und Soldat,* which took a much more openly revolutionary socialist position. Given the much larger communist party operation, it is hard to compare their effectiveness - although assessments of effectiveness depend on your objective - another debate for another day. Until 1944, both operations only managed to attract individual German soldiers, most of whom were betrayed and executed or deported. But the story of Albert Hauser gives an example the relationship between indigenous French Resistance and German antifascist soldiers. Albert Hauser, worked with the French resistance in Dijon until the Gestapo caught him. He was sent to forced labour building the V2 bunkers in the North. He escaped during an air-raid and was found by a French peasant wondering in her fields. She moved him on to the French underground, who nursed him back to health and, following discussions with the German section of MOI, dispatched him to join a resistance group near Clermont l'Hérault and he participated in the liberation of Montpellier.[10]

But the *Travail Allemand* did not start as a formal KPD initiative. Wally Heckling and

8 Guillon, Jean-Marie, 1989, "Les Étrangers dans la Résistance provençale." *Revue D'histoire Moderne Et Contemporaine*, vol. 36, no. 4, pp. 658–671.
9 Ville de Brignoles, n/d, *J'étais là et je me souviens de la Libération de Brignoles...*, Archives Municipales de Brignoles
10 Hauser, Albert, n/d, "A la croisée des chemins", Document, ARC 1000-No.31, Paris: Institute d'histoire du temps présent.

Lispeth Peterson, two German comrades in exile in Paris decided on their own initiative not to join the mass exodus when the German Army arrived in 1940, but managed to get jobs in a German company's offices in Paris and supply false papers to active fighters, to get jobs for those facing deportation and supply information to the Allies. Only later were they incorporated into the "official" TA structure. There was scepticism at first among the KPD leadership in France. Franz Dahlem, one of the communist leaders in the internment camps, thought the idea suicidal, particularly as many of the volunteers were of Jewish heritage, and he argued that the party had lost so many militants in Germany that everyone was needed to rebuild a democratic Germany after the war. He refused to escape from the internment camp at Gurs, from where he was suddenly deported to Malthausen KZ along with hundreds of others. Dora Schaul, a German communist of Jewish heritage interned the camp at Berns, was discouraged from escaping by the KPD leadership in the camp, but as she said in an interview in 1998, "We escaped nevertheless". This was just as well because the Jewish internees were soon deported to die in the death camps. Dora escaped to Lyon where she worked in the *Wehrmacht* post office opposite the Klaus Barbie's office. This enabled her to keep tabs on the comings and goings of the Gestapo and inform the Lyon resistance.[11]

These deportations gave a majority to those seeking to infiltrate and subvert the German war effort and the TA was formally established, led by Otto Niebergall for the KPD, Franz Marek for the Austrian Communist Party (KPÖ) and Arthur London for the Czechoslovak party (KSČ). But there was heavy price to pay for this activity and over 100 TA activists, mainly women, were executed or died in deportation. Mindla Djament was one of the first victims; arrested in July 1942 on the demarcation line between then occupied and unoccupied France while she was transporting propaganda leaflets, she was sent to Germany and executed in Breslau on July 3, 1944. In Marseilles, Irene Wosikowski made

Dora Schaul

contact with a German sailor, Herman Frischalowski, who declared himself ready to distribute anti-nazi leaflets. She went to the rendezvous he had set on 26th July 1943 near the Marseilles zoo with some propaganda material, but the sailor had betrayed her and she was arrested by the German police and security forces (Sipo-SD). She was guillotined in

11 Collin, Claude. "Dora Schaul, Renée Fabre Dans La Résistance (1913-1999)." *Guerres Mondiales Et Conflits Contemporains*, no. 194 (1999): 187-93. Collin, Claude. "le TRAVAIL ALLEMAND: origines et filiations." *Guerres Mondiales Et Conflits Contemporains*, no. 230 (2008): 125-36.

Berlin on 27th October 1944.[12]

The constant transfers to the Eastern Front meant were an additional difficulty, as this made it difficult for the activists to build up reliable contacts. Nevertheless, there was some success. Lieutenant Hans Heisel recalls lending his Luger automatic pistol to the FTP-MOI to assassinate SS Standartenführer Von Ritter who headed the German side of the STO forced labour operation. Walter Kramer, a Corporal in Toulouse, sometime member of the SPD, was able to warn of Gestapo raids, distributed tracts amongst his fellow soldiers and used the regimental mail to send propaganda back into Germany. Gerhard Leo found a job as an interpreter in the transport centre in Toulouse, a job which gave him access to full details of the troop movements in the area and which he passed on to his contacts in the resistance. Berthold Blanc from Leipzig deserted in Toulouse, complete with arms and ammunition, and fought with the Maquis until he was killed in the battle for Espéraza in the South of France. Hans Heisel, Kurt Hälker and Arthur Eberhard worked in the communication department of headquarters of the German Navy in Paris, from where they were able to pass on a wealth of sensitive information. When the uprising that liberated Paris broke out in 1944, they deserted with their weapons and joined the insurgents. Hans Heisel was proud to say that he helped defend the HQ of the French Communist Party. It was not all propaganda and information gathering, Max Brings blew up the *Wehrmacht* officers mess in Nice, killing a large number of *Wehrmacht* and SS officers.[13] There are a considerable number of individual histories of this sort, but in the case of serving German soldiers, the rebellion seems to have only been on an individual basis. The Austrian section of the TA had greater success and a group of Austrian soldiers in the *Wehrmacht* changed sides during the insurrection in Paris in 1944, while a considerable number of Austrian soldiers on the Eastern Front deserted to the Red Army and showed TA leaflets as evidence of their *bona-fides*.[14]

By 1943, the losses on the Eastern front resulted in the German government taking two decisions to compensate for their lack of manpower, the forced recruitment of labour from France and the recruitment of non-German soldiers into the *Waffen-SS*. Both these measures would have unintended detrimental effects on the German war effort.

From mid-1942, there was a mass rural revolt in France and the guerrillas were just the armed spearhead of a mass movement. The trigger for this revolt was the *Service du Travail Obligatoire* (STO), the requisition of forced labour to work in Germany, which caused thousands of young men to flee into the country where they were sheltered by the rural population. There was a severe shortage of labour in the country as a million and a half French soldiers were still being held in German POW camps. The *réfactaires*, as those

---

12 Bonte, Florimond, *Les Antifacistes allemands dans la Résistance*, Paris: Éditions sociales, 1969, pp. 303-306
13 Perrault, Gilles, *Taupes Rouges contre SS*, Paris: Messidor, 1986.
14 Joutard, Philippe & Marcot, François, 1992, *Les étrangers dans la Résistance en France*, Besançon: Musée de la Résistance et de la Déportation, p.91.

fleeing the STO were called, were sheltered in the country in return for their labour on the farms and it was a natural step to supporting them in the hills and forests when the Vichy authorities came looking for them. In turn it was logical for these *réfactaires* to arm themselves against the forces of repression. They then quickly turned from defence to attack, from being the hunted to the hunters. This was a milieu that welcomed the Spanish, German, Yugoslav, Italian and Jewish veterans of the International Brigades as they had a common enemy in the German and Italian occupation forces along with their French fascist allies while their previous military experience was much appreciated. The use of the term "Jewish" needs a word of explanation in the context of the Resistance. There were French citizens of Jewish heritage, some of whom fought in the general French Resistance, Raymond and Lucie Aubrac are perhaps the most celebrated, while others, mainly Zionists, were engaged in specifically Jewish organisations. Then there were the Yiddish-speaking immigrant workers from Central Europe who had been forced underground by the anti-Semitic, xenophobic round-ups and internments; these were organised principally in the Yiddish speaking section of the FTP-MOI. Finally, and this group are mainly of concern to our investigation, there were the Jewish German refugees and exiles , most of whom would have thought of themselves as communists or socialists first, Germans second and Jewish third. Just because the Nazi authorities had stripped this group of their German citizenship, does not mean that we should deny them the honour of seeing them as internationalist traitors.

The German authorities certainly saw the situation as a rural revolt and treated the peasants in the villages with extreme brutality. There was a general policy of burning villages and massacring civilians in areas of strong Maquis activity in an attempt to terrorise the base of support of the guerrilla bands. For example, having failed to catch some resistance fighters in an isolated village in the Cervennes because the rebels had received a tip-off from a friendly Gendarme, the German Army burnt most of the village and took three men and a woman back to Nimes, where they publicly hanged them in the town centre. In this brutal war, the civilian supporters were just as much in the front line as the fighters in the hills and this affected women particularly. In the cemetery of Alès in the Gard are two tombstones recording the murders of, Hedwig Robens et Lisa Ost: "*Partisane allemande, morte pour la liberté, assassinée par le Gestapo*".[15] These two German women, formerly of the International Brigades, were acting as a courier and a nurse for the local maquis when they were picked up in an SS raid on the village of Nozières in which they were staying, taken to prison in Alés, where they were tortured and killed by the German security service.

In the densely wooded hills and mountains of the Morvan in western Burgundy, the Haute-Savoi region in the east and the southern reaches of the Massif Central, particularly

15 "German Partisan, died for freedom, murdered by the Gestapo".

the Cervennes region of Averyon, Lozere and Tarn, the main antipartisan action was conducted by German forces, *Wehrmacht* and SS, along with their French fascist auxiliaries in the *Milice*. Of the German forces, three-quarters of the *Waffen-SS* were not German citizens. By the middle of 1943, the German armed forces were facing a serious manpower shortage and, as a result, started recruiting non-German men. There were Poles and Czechs forcibly conscripted from their occupied territories, as well as Yugoslav Muslims from Bosnia, who had joined more or less willingly in the belief that this would ensure German protection from oppression by their Catholic Croat neighbours. Ferid Dzanic and Bozo Jelinek, were sent by the Yugoslav Partisans to join the 13th Handzar Division of the SS, a mainly Bosnian Muslim unit, that by mid-1943 was stationed in Villefranche-de-Rouergue in the Aveyron region of Southern France. These two militants were able to organise a rebellion on the 17 September 1943 and Lieutenant Kirschbaum, the battalion commander was taken prisoner and, along with other officers, was shot. However, the Battalion Mufti (Muslim religious leader) managed to warn loyal SS troops and the mutiny was suppressed with most of the rebels being executed. Nevertheless, a considerable number did escape with the help of the local residents and most then fought with the Resistance till the end of the war.[16]

However, by far the largest contingent of non-German members of the SS were former citizens of the Soviet Union. In mid-August 1944, with the US forces advancing across France, the predominantly Ukrainian 102nd and 118th Battalions of the 30th *Waffen Grenadier* Division of the SS were shipped to Haut-Savoie in Eastern France. Some were nationalists who had joined to resist what they saw as Soviet occupation of the Ukraine, others had been in the Red Army, captured while fighting against the Germans and ending up in a prison camp. Some had done both. The only future for them was either serving in the SS or a short brutish existence with a likely violent death in the POW camps, where one and a half million Soviet POWs were deliberately starved to death. Whatever their reasons for joining, they had little interest in fighting in France, while their German officers treated them with racist contempt. The senior Ukrainian officer, Major Lev Hloba made contact with the local forces of the French Resistance and planned their mutiny. While marching through the Savoy countryside, Lev Hloba shouted the order "Helmets on" and, as the German officers' and NCOs' hands were occupied obeying the order, the Ukrainians shot them or beat them to death. The German dead numbered some 394, including nearly 100 officers, and 820 Ukrainians then joined the waiting French Resistance and fought alongside them till the end of the war.[17]

---

16 Lepre, George, *Himmler's Bosnian Division: The Waffen-SS Handschar Division 1943–1945*. Atglen, Philadelphia: Schiffer Publishing, 1997.
17 Rohde, M. *When Eternities Met: A True Story of Terror, Mutiny, Loss, and Love in a Disremembered Second World War*, Union Bridge, Maryland: Pencil and Barn, 2017;
Kosyk, Wolodymyr, *Les Ukrainiens dans la Résistance francaise*, Paris: Publications de l'Est Européen, 1994.

In July 1944, in Carmaux, the town that Jean Jaurès had represented before the First World War, the local FTP, which was predominately composed of Polish miners but already reinforced with 60 deserters from the *Wehrmacht*, ex-Red Army POWs from Kazakhstan, called for an insurrectional general strike. In the ensuing battle, women from the Polish mining families approached a group of Georgian soldiers in the German Army to persuade them to change sides. This they did, taking their German officers with them as prisoners. Altogether 185 ex-Red Army fighters took part in the battle for the liberation of Carmaux and the surrounding region.

A purist may say that, despite wearing German uniforms, these people were not strictly speaking traitors as they were not ethnic Germans, so let us finish with some who were. Otto Kühne was a communist railway worker who had been elected as a Reichstag deputy. He fled to France where he was interned as an undesirable alien in a labour camp, working as a wood-cutter. In 1943, the resistance got word that these wood-cutters were about to be rounded up and deported. Otto Kühne and about 40 of his comrades, mainly German veterans of the International Brigades fled into the Cervennes mountains. The Cervennes are a traditionally protestant region of France with their own history of persecution and exile, which enabled the local people to empathise with the German exiles. Most of what we know of this group we have from Pierre Chaptal, a young protestant clergyman who fought with them, as they joked, "With a bible in one hand and a pistol in the other". Initially they were quite prepared to kill Germans but were reluctant to kill French fascist militiamen; it was the clergyman who convinced them that they were fighting fascism no matter of what nationality. In the Cervennes, the German Army supported by the Vichy Gendarmerie and Milice only controlled the main roads. Whenever they ventured onto the minor roads, they risked ambush. The German Army did make several large raids into the forests to attack the Maquis camps, but were frequently beaten off with much loss of life. But not always and when the SS attacked the Bir-Hakeim maquis group at La Parade, 59 guerrillas were killed including a dozen Germans from Otto Kühne's detachment, many of the dead having been tortured and killed after surrendering.

Germans were an important part of the battle for the town of Nîmes, where Norbert Beisäcker was given the honour of taking down the swastika flag from the town hall. Martin Kalb, who led the German fighters in the battle for Nîmes is pictured in the front rank as they marched in the parade to celebrate the Liberation, with Norbert Beisäcker carrying the French Tricolor. Otto Kühne himself was appointed Colonel and led a force of 2000 fighters, mainly French, but including a significant number of Armenian deserters from the SS *Ost-Legion* who had mutinied.[18]

On July 14th, 1994, the fiftieth anniversary of the liberation of Paris, President François

---

18 Brès, Evelyne et Yvan, *Un maquis d'antifascistes allemands en France (1942-1944)*, Montpellier: Les Presses du Languedoc.

Mitterrand invited the German Chancellor of the time, Helmut Kohl, to attend the parade, in which German military personnel of the Eurocorps were participating. At the request of French Resistance associations, the government had agreed to forward to the Federal authorities a list of German citizens who had participated in the Resistance in France. Helmut Kohl refused to allow them on the platform and Paris did not insist. So two German veterans of the French Resistance stood on the pavement wearing their French medals as the German troops marched by.[19]

German Maquisards marching in the Liberation Day parade through Nîmes

19 Jean Morawski, "Peter Gingold : le drapeau blanc de la victoire", *L'Humanité*, 12 juillet 1994.

Ilio Barontini

Tobias Abse

Ilio Barontini (1890-1951) was an extraordinary figure, playing an important role in the Spanish Civil War, the organisation of Ethiopian resistance to the Italian occupation, the French Resistance and the Italian Resistance. No Italian Communist of his generation was involved in military struggles against both Italian Fascism and its Spanish and German allies on so many different geographical fronts.

Barontini was born in Cecina, a town to the south of Livorno, but his family moved to the city of Livorno during his youth. He came from a left-wing family; his father had been an Anarchist in his youth. He joined the Partito Socialista Italiano in Livorno in 1914, becoming a City Councillor in November 1920. He joined the Partito Comunista d'Italia (PCd'I) at its foundation in 1921, personally securing the Teatro San Marco in Livorno as the venue for its founding congress. He played a leading role within Livornese Communism, acting as Inter-Provincial Secretary for Livorno and Pisa, and standing in the 1921 Parliamentary election. After the Fascists took power in 1922, he inevitably paid a high price for his political activity. He was arrested in 1923 and 1925, but was acquitted on both occasions. He was arrested again in July 1927 and spent a year in prison, but was acquitted by the Special Tribunal as a result of vehemently denying that he was still a PCd'I member. In reality he resumed his role as head of the Communist Underground in Livorno as soon as he was released.

Eventually, on 1 May 1931, he escaped by boat with a group of other Livornese Communists to Corsica, from where he made his way to mainland France. The PCd'I gave him the role of chief organiser amongst the Italian Communist political refugees in France, procuring false identity documents, finding safe accommodation, securing suitable venues for clandestine meetings and so forth. This was the height of the Third Period of the Comintern, and the PCd'I, believing the final downfall of Fascism was imminent, sent a large number of comrades back into Italy, only to find they were very frequently arrested within days of their arrival. Barontini was rather unfairly blamed for these disasters, and as a result he was sent to the Soviet Union in 1932, as a punishment rather than a promotion.

Barontini soon secured an important role in the Profintern, dealing with Italian sailors visiting Soviet ports, as well as acting as the Secretary in charge of Italian political immigrants, but his refusal to move from Moscow to Odessa in October 1933 led to a long period as a production worker in an aircraft factory. In 1936 Barontini was sent to Spain and this period from November 1936 until September 1937 gave rise to his heroic reputation. His main role in the International Brigades was as a political commissar of the Garibaldi Battalion (Garibaldi Brigade after April 1937), three quarters of whom were Italian antifascists. He was Acting Battalion Commander during the Battle of Guadalajara in March 1937 where the largest contingent on the Francoist side were the 35,000 Italian Fascist troops. It was the first time that the Italian Fascist Expeditionary Force was defeated by the Spanish Republicans. The fact that the Garibaldi Battalion was involved in direct combat with Italian Fascist troops and they were victorious on their section of the Front, was of enormous symbolic importance, raising the morale of the whole Italian anti-Fascist movement in Italy and abroad, and giving rise to the slogan: "Today in Spain, tomorrow in Italy". Barontini's recall from Spain in September 1937 seems to have been largely due to a decision by the PCd'I's leader and Comintern Representative in Spain, Palmiro Togliatti, who had a low opinion of Barontini's performance as a political Commissar, claiming he was too ready to yield to the demands of non-Communists.

After little more than a year back in France, Barontini was sent to Ethiopia in late 1938, where he remained until June 1940 acting as an advisor and trainer of Ethiopian rebels engaged in guerrilla warfare against the Italian occupying troops. He had only two Italian Communist veterans of the Spanish Civil War as his assistants, and once the Italian Colonial authorities became aware of their presence, a price was put on the head of these dangerous Italian subversives, even if their real identity was never uncovered.

Ilio Barontini in Ethiopia

Back in Paris, he trained members of the French Resistance in bomb making. Then, after the German invasion of the Soviet Union, he was sent south to Marseilles, where he played a leading role in urban guerrilla warfare, organising bombings of the German troops in a hotel near the train station, in a queue of German soldiers outside a brothel, and on a tram that was supposed to transport German soldiers from the Vieux Port. These actions led the French Communist Party to put Barontini in charge of a network of urban guerrillas recruited from Spanish and Armenian immigrants as well as his Italian associates.

By October 1943, Barontini was back in Italy. He played the leading role in the Italian Resistance in Emilia Romagna. In the light of his Marseille experience, he favoured urban guerrilla operations rather than attempts to liberate large rural zones from the German occupation. The most famous exploit he led was the Battle of Porta Lame, inside the walls of Bologna, on 7 November 1944, in which he led 300 partisans against 1500 German Nazis and Italian Fascists, killing 216 of the enemy at the cost of only 12 Resistance fighters. Naturally, Barontini was also involved in the final victory in Bologna on 21 April 1945, a few days before similar Partisan insurrections in Milan, Genoa and Turin.

After the end of the war, Barontini finally returned to his native Livorno, where he once again became Secretary of the Livornese Communist Federation, and was elected, first to the Constituent Assembly in 1946 and then to the Senate in 1948. On 22 January 1951, Barontini died in a car accident near Scandicci, on the way to a Communist Party Congress in Florence.

Supporting the Enemy in the Death Agony of French Colonialism

Ian Birchall

Introduction

In 1945, at the Liberation, France still had the second largest colonial empire in the world. Twenty years later most of it was gone. France has retained major economic interests in Africa and made repeated military interventions there,[1] but the crude brutality of direct colonial rule is gone for good. The end of colonialism involved two long and disastrous wars, in Indochina and Algeria. The Algerian war in particular tore through the very heart of French society, leading to the collapse of the Fourth Republic.

France was a deeply divided society. It had just emerged from four years of German occupation. What is often referred to, somewhat misleadingly, as the "French Resistance" was in fact to a considerable extent a civil war. The Nazis had many enthusiastic collaborators, sometimes keener in their anti-Semitism than the Germans. When the war ended many Resisters joined the regular army – and discovered the reality of colonial life, where the indigenous inhabitants were often treated very much as the French had been under the Nazis.

Decolonisation exposed other deep divisions in French society. Contrary to the views of some latter-day "Leninists" there was no compelling economic reason for France to maintain its empire; the years of the loss of empire coincided with the "*Trente glorieuses*" - the thirty glorious years of the post-war boom, marked by full employment and rising living standards. Some sections of French capitalism could accommodate easily to the loss of empire; while the Algerian war still continued the Renault management were having talks with the Algerian National Liberation Front (FLN), probably about potential car sales in independent Algeria.[2]

So the division about colonial policy was not a simple left-right one. The myth of France's "civilising mission" was widespread, and closely bound up with republicanism and the principles of secularism – *laïcité*. (Jules Ferry, the architect of secular education, had also played a key role in the colonisation of Indochina.) So the parties of the left, the Socialists and even to some extent the Communists, were deeply ambiguous about the colonial question.

A divided society was ripe for treason. Even the concept of the "national interest" was sharply contested. So during the colonial wars there were some individuals who reached out to the other side.

---

1 See for example "Where France Would Intervene Next in Africa", at https://worldview.stratfor.com/article/where-france-would-intervene-next-africa (accessed 4/9/2018).
2 Clara and Henri Benoîts, 2014, *L'Algérie au coeur*, Paris: Éditions Syllepse, p99.

Indochina

Independence for Indochina was possible in 1945, which would have made not one, but two wars unnecessary. Ho Chi Minh was ready to take over, while the French were not yet prepared to reoccupy. But Attlee's Labour government sent troops which held the territory till France was able to recolonise – a fact generally ignored by those who want to stress the positive achievements of the 1945 government.

After failed negotiations war broke out in November 1946 when the French fleet bombarded Haiphong. For the first six months of the war the Communist Party (PCF) was still in government, and the main opposition came from the Trotskyists and the Socialist Party youth. But when the Cold War began and the PCF was excluded from government they turned to a militant campaign of action against what they rightly called the 'dirty war'. (Though what a clean war might look like is a more tricky question.) The war dragged on till 1954, when the fall of the allegedly impregnable fortress of Dien Bien Phu meant the end of French rule in Indochina; the Geneva agreements partitioned Vietnam, preparing the way for another war.

Opposition to the war was substantial, and overflowed parliamentary channels. Dockers systematically refused to load or unload ships conveying supplies for Indochina. This began with dockers in Algeria and rapidly spread to Marseille and ports throughout France. The strikes were paralleled by vigorous demonstrations in which military supplies were unloaded and damaged.[3] A young woman was jailed for lying down on railway lines in front of a train carrying material for Indochina.[4] In 1950 it was claimed that 60 per cent of war material arriving in Indochina had been sabotaged in some way, though the government denied these figures.[5] The war was unpopular: after 1947 there were never more than 27% who thought the solution was to send more troops; by 1953 35% favoured a negotiated peace and another 15% wanted the troops brought home straight away.[6]

This atmosphere of near civil war obviously had an impact on the troops in Indochina. The political instability of the Fourth Republic meant that no government dared to send conscripts to Indochina. Thus the war was fought by the regular army, into which the Resistance militias had been integrated. Then there was the Foreign Legion, a particularly obnoxious outfit which at this time consisted largely of Germans who were glad to be at the other side of the world if their wartime conduct were to be investigated. There were also soldiers recruited in North Africa, and native Indochinese troops.[7]

It was a brutish army fighting a brutal war. French soldiers were told that the Geneva

---

3 Ruscio, Alain, 1985, *Les communistes français et la guerre d'Indochine 1944-1954*, Paris, pp.241-3, 251-3, 257-8.
4 *Ibid.*, pp253-5.
5 Dalloz, Jacques, 1987, *La Guerre d'Indochine*, Paris, p.169.
6 Ruscio, *Les communistes français et la guerre d'Indochine*, p.200.
7 See Doyon, Jacques, 1973, *Les soldats blancs de Hô Chi Minh*, Paris.

Conventions applied to regular armies, but not to "outlaws" and "terrorists" like the Vietminh.[88] (The Nazis had said much the same about the French Resistance.) There was widespread use of torture and random killing of civilians. But there were also quite a few Communists in the army. The PCF positively encouraged its members to serve in the army, and this did not change as the war evolved. PCF members were very firmly told that they must not desert, become conscientious objectors or seek in any way to evade or resign from military service.

But if the PCF was clear to the point of dogmatism on the necessity for its members to serve in Indochina, it was far less clear what they were to do there. Communist soldiers had various choices:

- to try and ensure that the war was fought reasonably humanely and to attempt to prevent atrocities:
- to argue against the war with their fellow soldiers:
- to take positive action to sabotage the war effort:
- to provide information - or even supplies - to the Viet Minh.

The concrete possibilities of all these were limited and mutually contradictory. A soldier claiming to represent the interests of his fellows would hardly enhance his credibility if he were seen to be responsible for sending them into battle with defective weapons. And anyone giving material assistance to the enemy would have to assume a pose of political orthodoxy in order to divert suspicion from himself. Communists were strongly discouraged from aiding the "enemy" - when André Marty, who was in charge of the PCF's military work, was told of a group of Communist soldiers who were supplying arms to the Viet Minh, he flew in a rage and called them provocateurs.[9] In addition known Communists sometimes fell victim to bullets from their own side.[10]

There was quite a significant level of desertion during the war. But of the total 30,000 or more deserters the vast majority were Vietnamese troops. Of the two or three hundred French soldiers who went over to the Vietminh, most did so primarily for personal reasons, to escape punishment or in order to marry a Vietnamese woman.[11] However, there were a small number of French soldiers (and also Germans from the French Foreign Legion) who went over to the Vietminh on the basis of political conviction. I'll look at just two examples.

8 Jean-Luc Einaudi, 2001, *Viêt-Nam! La Guerre d'Indochine (1945-1954)*, Paris: Jean-Luc Einaudi, Viêt-Nam! La Guerre d'Indochine, p.59.
9 Ruscio, *Les communistes français et la guerre d'Indochine*, p.374.
10 Dalloz, *La Guerre d'Indochine*, p.169.
11 Ruscio, *Les communistes français et la guerre d'Indochine*, p.375.

Albert Clavier[12]

Albert Clavier, born in 1927, was too young for any serious involvement in the Resistance; his elder brother was a Communist and survived a spell in Buchenwald. At the Liberation, hoping to see something of the world, he enrolled in the Colonial Artillery – though as he recalled, he "didn't know much about what the colonies were". Since he had a girl-friend and an elderly mother, he regretted the decision, but was unable to avoid being sent to Indochina. On the boat there were a number of Foreign Legion soldiers, some of them former Nazis. A stop at Djibouti (then part of French Somaliland) revealed to him the enormous contrast between wealth and poverty in a colonial territory.

On arrival in Indochina he made friends with a Vietnamese family who were probably Vietminh sympathisers. He also observed a fellow-soldier being beaten to death by members of the Foreign Legion for being a Communist. He observed other French atrocities and made friends with a Vietnamese teacher who was a Vietminh supporter. He decided to defect to the Vietminh, though he made it clear he was not prepared to bear arms against his compatriots. A fake kidnapping was arranged and he went over – he was subsequently condemned to death.

He was employed on propaganda work, addressing French troops with a loud-speaker and urging them to lay down their arms, making parallels between the Vietnamese struggle and the French Resistance. He also worked with French prisoners of war, but little was achieved. Later he worked with the French-language service of the Vietminh radio station.

He also worked with defectors who had come over to the Vietminh. But this was not a fruitful field of activity. Many of those who had deserted from the French forces had done so, not from any political conviction, but because they were accused of some criminal offence – theft, rape or murder. As a result there was little interest in the courses of political education provided. There was, however, some success with Arab prisoners, some of whom later joined the FLN in Algeria.

Clavier shared the living standards of his Vietnamese hosts, and ate nothing but two bowls of rice per day. He married a Vietnamese woman, and after a divorce married another.

Georges Boudarel[13]

Georges Boudarel was brought up in a Catholic family, but became a Communist under the influence of a fellow-worker while working as a supervisor in a lycée in the immediate post-war period. He does not seem to have been a particularly active or sophisticated member, and when, in the late 1940s, he applied for a teaching post in Indochina, his PCF

---

12 See Collin, Claude, 2011, *De la Résistance à la guerre d'Indochine*, Paris: Indes Savantes, pp.147-90.
13 See Einaudi, *Viêt-Nam!*

contacts told him to drop his Party membership since the Party did not organise abroad. As he recounted, "I was advised to leave my membership card in France and not to present myself as a Party member." But he was put in touch with the banned Marxist Cultural Group in Saigon.[14]

Boudarel spent some time teaching in Vietnam and Laos, and became sympathetic to the indigenous population. In 1950 he defected to the Vietminh (had he not done so he would have been called up for military service in France, though not, of course, to fight in Indochina). In so doing he was aware that he was acting against the explicit advice of the PCF.

Boudarel was accepted by the Vietminh, who used him for various jobs. Like Clavier, he did not take arms against his compatriots. He had to adapt himself to a tough lifestyle, travelling long distances through the Vietnamese jungle. He worked for some time on a Vietminh radio station, and then became political education officer in camp 113, a prisoner of war camp for captured French troops. There are differing accounts of his activity here. He denies having given long lectures and says he attempted to organise discussions.

One prisoner recalled:

> We talked about politics in general, reasons for the war, what was wrong with it, what was going on in France, the opposition to the war in France, the slogans: 'Peace in Vietnam by bringing home the expeditionary force', etc. There was absolutely no question of indoctrination ... we never had L'Humanité [daily paper of the French Communist Party] in the camp. There was nothing at all. The only time we had newspapers, I can't remember which, we used pages to roll cigarettes.'[15]

He was obliged to retain a considerable distance from the prisoners, many of whom regarded him with suspicion and distrust. French prisoners who were in the camp concede that he never used physical violence towards them, but believe he must share responsibility for the conditions in the camp where there was a very high death rate among prisoners. However, the prevalence of disease and the shortage of medicines were an integral part of the situation and were out of his control. The Vietnamese themselves were short of food and medication, and shared what drugs they had with the prisoners, who suffered because they were unaccustomed to the climate.

After the amnesty in the 1960s Boudarel returned to France and, using his knowledge of the language and culture of Vietnam, pursued an academic career.

Algeria

Indochina was remote, but Algeria was close – and constitutionally it was an integral

14 *Ibid*. p.8.
15 Einaudi, *Việt-Nam!*, p.206.

part of the French state. But while the settlers had full rights as French citizens, the indigenous population were legally subjects, not citizens. France boasted of its "civilising mission", but after a century of French rule the Muslim population had an 85 per cent illiteracy rate.[16]

In 1954 after Dien Bien Phu, younger militants in the nationalist movement formed the FLN (National Liberation Front); on 1 November 1954 the FLN launched a wave of synchronised attacks across Algeria. The war raged for seven and a half years (though it was only in 1999 that it was officially recognised that it had been a war). Under pressure from angry settlers Socialist Party Prime Minister Mollet abandoned any attempts at making peace and instead set out to crush the rebellion. By the end of 1956 there were 450,000 French troops in Algeria. There was considerable resistance from reservists and conscripts, but these revolts got no support from any section of the mainstream left. In March 1956 the National Assembly voted for 'special powers' to crush the revolt; PCF deputies gave their backing. The French Army was increasingly guilty of systematic abuses, in particular torture and the killing of prisoners.

The constitutionally fragile Fourth Republic, based on a series of coalition governments, could not stand the pressure of war. In May 1958 there was a military-settler rising in Algeria, and the Fourth Republic collapsed amidst threats of 'civil war'. General Charles de Gaulle, a veteran right-wing military leader from World War II, took over the government on the basis of a referendum which established a Fifth Republic with a new constitution. De Gaulle's main aim was to defend the interests of French capitalism, for which the preservation of colonial rule in Algeria was no longer necessary. In strictly military terms the FLN was not progressing, but at the same time the war was becoming intolerable to more and more sections of the French population. By March 1959 71% favoured ceasefire negotiations with the FLN.[17] By 1961 it was clear that de Gaulle had no alternative to negotiating with the FLN. In March 1962 an agreement was signed; this was put to a referendum in April and was approved by over 90 per cent of those voting. Algeria became fully independent on 5 July 1962.

The appalling role of the Socialist Party and even the Communist Party had led to the emergence of a significant current to the left of both parties, and this was the milieu within which activists gave concrete support to the 'enemy'. At the outbreak of the war there were over 200,000 Algerian workers in mainland France, usually doing unpleasant and low-paid jobs. By 1962 the figure had more than doubled, with Algerians often replacing French workers who had been conscripted to fight in Algeria.

These Algerian workers were an essential source of financial support for the FLN, who

16 Evans, Martin, 2012, *Algeria: France's Undeclared War*, Oxford: OUP, p.112.
17 *Ibid*. p.257.

levied a tax on them. But to transport this money they needed European supporters not liable to be victims of the racist stop and search methods of the French police. These were what became known as the *porteurs de valises* – suitcase carriers. I'll give three examples of concrete support for the FLN.

Henri and Clara Benoîts[18]

Henri and Clara Benoîts worked at Renault Billancourt, the heart of the French car industry, throughout the period of the Algerian war. Both had a deep political commitment. Henri, a draughtsman, became a Trotskyist at the age of eighteen and remained a lifelong revolutionary. Asked years later what motivated his actions during the war, he wrote: "Class feeling must have precedence over national feeling. This war of Algerians against the colonial system, and *not* against French people, was therefore profoundly just in its aims..... since the practice of unity is the basis of common action, it seemed to me that any blow against my enemy, French capitalism, could only help to weaken it and encourage the struggle of the working class against its exploiters."[19] Clara, originally a shorthand-typist, had Hungarian parents; her great-uncle was killed in Auschwitz, and her uncle died fighting in Spain. She was a member of the Communist Party; she remained one, though highly critical, till 1970.

In the 1950s Billancourt had around forty thousand workers, of whom about ten per cent were North African, mainly Algerian. These were mainly concentrated in the foundries and on the assembly lines. Many were active in the main union, the CGT, and some were in the Communist Party, though they left after the vote for "special powers". In this situation "suitcase carrying" began almost spontaneously. As Clara related: "When an Algerian comrade thought that the cops were going to his home, he gave me his keys so I could go and remove some compromising packets .... Odd jobs like that on the personal level."[20]

Henri explained later:

> You must remember that at this time there were frequent police checks conducted on a racial basis in the streets and the underground stations. Somebody walking along with a packet, if they had an Algerian face, was more likely to be stopped. It was so easy to ask a bloke or a woman from your shop: 'Take this, I'm in danger of being caught.' This was probably the sort of assistance which French people, more numerous than is often thought, offered. Ladlani, who was in charge of the FLN French Federation at the time, told us recently [October 1991] that if anyone had tried to make a serious calculation of the number of acts of solidarity by French people with their Algerian workmates, there would probably be several thousands.

18 See Benoîts, *L'Algérie au coeur*.
19 Benoîts, *L'Algérie au coeur*, p.183.
20 Benoîts, Clara and Henri, "The Algerian War Seen from Renault-Billancourt", *Revolutionary History* Vol. 10, No. 4 (2012), p.131.

These are actions which cannot be measured but which still show that racism had not become universal.[21]

Subsequently formal contacts were made between the Fourth International and the FLN, involving Michel Pablo [Michalis N. Raptis, a leader of the Fourth International] and Mohammed Harbi, later a distinguished historian. Comrades did a variety of jobs assisting the FLN with the production and distribution of literature. On one occasion they got eleven large suitcases containing pages of *El Moudjahid*, the FLN newspaper to the editorial team of which Frantz Fanon belonged. They had to sit up all night collating these, then go to work the next morning.

The kind of small victory that could be won in a well-organised workplace was shown by the case of Abdelghani Ben Nacef:

Security staff came into the workshop and his foreman came to ask him to go to the office. He understood that the presence of factory security staff asking him to go with them to the personnel office was not normal. He refused to follow them. He thought 'they're trying to arrest me' and he went to find Ziani who was the forge delegate in the next workshop. Immediately the workers in the forge stopped work, booed the security staff and said 'clear out of the factory, no security in our workshop'. What is important, is that at this time in the forges the great majority of the workers were French, skilled workers, sometimes ranked as management because their pay was sometimes more than double. They were a labour 'aristocracy', but with a pronounced sense of class... The Algerian workers from the foundries and the mainly French workers from the forges united to drive out the security and Ghani hid in the factory...What happened next is also interesting: Ziani came to tell me that 'the cops have come to arrest Ben Nacef, we must get him out'. It was payday. We had to get his clothes by breaking into his locker. This was done by Michel Eloy, the CGT delegate in the foundries supported by Claude Poperen, the general secretary of the CGT. The clothes were left at the factory committee office, and meanwhile, taking advantage of the lunch-break, I got him out of the factory and left him in Billancourt. We collected his pay by another Algerian borrowing Ghani's identity and I handed over everything [pay and clothes] to him. He then became clandestine.[22]

Clara, meanwhile, was active in a committee for peace in Algeria within the factory. This was broadly based and involved Communists and others. But as a Communist she was reprimanded by her party for calling for independence for Algeria rather than simply demanding peace, and for not saying enough about the fact that the war was against 'French interests'.

---

21 Benoîts, "The Algerian War Seen from Renault-Billancourt", p.134.
22 *Ibid.*, pp.135-36.

In October 1961 the FLN called a peaceful demonstration in protest at the curfew imposed on Algerians in Paris. Recognising that there might be trouble, the FLN asked Henri and Clara and other French sympathisers to act as observers; they were strictly instructed to observe but not to intervene in any circumstances.[23] In fact there was a police-organised massacre, in which up to two hundred Algerians died.

Francis Jeanson

Clara and Henri Benoîts carried suitcasesin their own workplace. Francis Jeanson[24] was active on a much broader stage. He had first visited Algeria as a young Resister during World War II. He spent another six months there in 1948 and met nationalist activists. At the same time he pursued quite a spectacular intellectual career. He wrote two books on Sartre and became managing editor of Sartre's journal *Les Temps modernes*, which as early as 1955 was urging conscripts to refuse to obey orders and to fraternise with the FLN.[25] He worked with Sartre on opposition to the war in Indochina (though he

Francis Jeanson

disagreed with him about the Hungarian rising of 1956). And in 1955 he and his wife Colette published *L'Algérie hors la loi* (Outlaw Algeria).[26] This was firmly partisan for the FLN – but also showed much greater knowledge of Algeria than most French politicians. They predicted the war would last eight years, that de Gaulle would use Algeria to return to power – and that Algeria would become independent, something that hardly anyone expected at this time.

Sartre's philosophy stressed the unity of theory and practice – for Jeanson practice came first: "I don't think there can be a practice derived from a theory. Practice always comes first; theory consolidates and rationalises things."[27] So in 1957 he abandoned his intellectual activities in order to devote himself to building a solidarity network; by April

23 Benoîts, *L'Algérie au coeur*, p.107.
24 See Marie-Pierre Ulloa, 2008, *Francis Jeanson: A Dissident Intellectual from the French Resistance to the Algerian War*, Bloomington, SUP.
25 [Editorial] 'L'Algérie n'est pas la France', *Les Temps modernes*, November 1955, pp.577-79.
26 Jeanson, Colette and Francis, 1955, *L'Algérie hors la loi*, Paris: Éditions du Seuil.
27 Ulloa, *Francis Jeanson*, p.145.

1958, just before de Gaulle's return, he had to become clandestine. As well as collecting money the Jeanson network sheltered FLN militants and published an illegal newspaper *Vérités Pour*. It was one of the four main networks, alongside the Fourth International, *La Voie communiste* and Henri Curiel's organisation.

Jeanson maintained his political independence; he worked with the FLN but never became a member. He argued against the FLN bombing campaign in mainland France in 1958, which he considered would be politically damaging. He was very critical of the Communist Party's position and hoped the Algerian war would transform the French left. In September 1960 the network was put on trial – without Jeanson who was still at liberty. The trial provided an opportunity for the launching of the Manifesto of the 121, which declared that "We respect and consider justified the actions of those French people who regard it as their duty to offer assistance and protection to Algerians oppressed in the name of the French people".[28] It was a major propaganda coup against the war. Jeanson was sentenced to ten years in jail – in absentia. And the Curiel network took over.

Fernand Iveton

The third example is rather different. It is often believed that the European settlers in Algeria were the most die-hard supporters of French rule. And indeed many of them were, but there was also a significant minority who supported the Algerian demand for independence. Frantz Fanon paid tribute to the many Europeans who supported the Algerian struggle, often at great cost to themselves: "The tortured European has behaved like an authentic militant in the national fight for independence."[29]

Fernand Iveton[30] was a poor settler who grew up in a Muslim quarter; there were close contacts between his family and their Muslim neighbours. His father was a Communist and he joined the Communist Party at the age of sixteen. He was employed in a gasworks and became a trade-union activist, where he tried to get unity of Muslim and European workers. He was recorded as having said to Muslim workers: "I'm a European, you're Muslims. There is no reason why you shouldn't have the same pay as me for doing the same work. You eat just as I do, and you pay the same price for goods."

When the FLN launched armed struggle in 1954 the Algerian Communist Party (PCA) was deeply divided. Originally, like the French party, it condemned "individual acts". But in June 1955 it took a secret decision to set up a military organisation, the "Combattants de la liberation" (fighters for liberation). The following year this merged with the FLN.[31] Iveton became a member.

28 For the text of the Manifesto and a list of signatories, see
https://www.marxists.org/history/france/algerian-war/1960/manifesto-121.htm (accessed 29/8/2018).
29 Fanon, Frantz, 1989, *Studies in a Dying Colonialism*, London, London: Earthscan, p.151.
30 See Jean-Luc Einaudi, *Pour l'exemple: l'affaire Fernand Iveton*, Paris, 1986.
31 On the Algerian CP see Drew, Allison, 2017, *We are no longer in France: Communists in colonial Algeria*, Manchester and New York: Manchester University Press.

In the spring of 1956 Iveton's friend, Henri Maillot, who had been called up into the army, stole a lorry-load of weapons and handed them over to the FLN. He was later captured and killed without trial. Then in September the FLN exploded two bombs in cafes in Algiers. Iveton opposed such indiscriminate acts because they implied that all Europeans were the enemy, and that the two communities were being driven apart. He was also concerned that some European chemistry students had helped the FLN manufacture the bombs.

He therefore resolved to take a different form of action; he seems to have done this on his own initiative and certainly without the approval of his party. He decided to plant a small bomb in his workplace, the Algiers gasworks. It was timed to explode at a time when it would have damaged property, but when no people would have been around to be injured; it was simply a symbolic gesture. In fact the bomb was discovered before it exploded.

Iveton was arrested and tortured. The trial took place within weeks of Iveton's arrest. The Communist Party did not provide him with a lawyer, so he had a rather ineffective legal defence. The Communist Parties in both France and Algeria were somewhat half-hearted in campaigning in his defence, and seemed to be divided as to what attitude to take to him.

Fernand Iveton with his wife Hélène and their son Jean-Claude

He was sentenced to death. On 6 February 1957 an appeal for mercy was heard by the *Conseil supérieur de la magistrature*. His lawyers had had only a few weeks to prepare a case; in an hour and a half twenty-one appeals were dealt with. The Justice Minister,

François Mitterrand voted to reject the appeal.[32]

The prospect of any significant number of settlers siding with the FLN was an alarming one and the government felt it necessary to act decisively. And the fact that Iveton was a Communist made it easier to denounce Communist influence on the FLN; this was important because the United States was unsympathetic to French colonialism, but if it could be argued that the fight against the FLN was a fight against communism, this might win American support. This was easier in the fiercely anti-Communist atmosphere following the Russian invasion of Hungary.

On 11 February 1957 Iveton was executed; a number of Algerians were executed at this time. Iveton was the only European among the 198 supporters of the FLN who were executed (as distinct to being killed in battle) during the war in Algeria.

Conclusion

It took France a long time to get over the violent way in which it had lost its empire. There was an amnesty in 1966 which enabled some of those involved to resume their lives. But the actions of those who deserted or carried suitcases has remained enormously controversial. Emmanuel Macron's recent rather ambiguous recognition that French colonialism was a "crime against humanity" may mark a shift in historical interpretation.[33] The fact remains that a few people said it at the time, and put their heads on the line to support the victims; if they had been heeded a great many lives would not have been lost needlessly.

Martin Evans conducted a series of interviews with former *porteurs de valises* between 1989 and 1995.[34] Several of those interviewed insisted that they were not traitors, and that they had in fact been acting patriotically. The publisher Jérôme Lindon, who published several books on French torture, stated "What I did, I did for France, not for Algeria" - and Evans notes that other interviewees "were adamant that they were not outsiders, beyond the boundaries of the national community, but insiders holding onto its core values".[35] Though in the eyes of the state all were guilty of treachery, there was a wide variation of motivations, and in many cases the term "treason" should be followed by a question mark.

In this period of French decolonisation, a whole number of people were prepared to risk their careers and ways of life in order to assist what were seen as the "enemy" - and to be rather more far-sighted than the professional politicians caught up in the pragmatism of power. They certainly saved the honour of France in one of the most disgraceful periods of its history.

---

32 On Mitterrand's (very dubious) role see Malye, François and Stora, Benjamin, 2010, *François Mitterrand et la guerre d'Algérie*, Paris: Calmann-Lévy.
33 See Eliza Anyangwe, "Brand new Macron, same old colonialism", *Guardian*, 11 July 2017.
34 Evans, Martin, 1997 *The Memory of Resistance: French opposition to the Algerian war (1954-1962)*, Oxford: Berg.
35 Evans, *The Memory of Resistance*, p.43.

Notes on Contributors

Tobias Abse did his doctoral research on the rise of fascism in Livorno. He was for many years a Lecturer in Modern European History at Goldsmiths College and has contributed articles on Italian politics and history to many publications, including *New Left Review, Socialist History* and *Weekly Worker*.

Ian Birchall is a socialist writer and translator. For many years he taught at Middlesex Polytechnic. He is the author of *The Spectre of Babeuf* (1997); *Sartre against Stalinism* (2004); *A rebel's Guide to Lenin* (2005) and *Tony Cliff: A Marxist for his Time* (2011). He has translated works by Alfred Rosmer and Victor Serge.

Steve Cushion is author of *The Hidden History of the Cuban Revolution: How the Working Class Shaped the Guerrillas' Victory; Killing Communists in Havana: The Start of the Cold War in Latin America* and *Up Down Turn Around: The Political Economy of Slavery*. He is joint author, with Dennis Bartholomew, of *By Our Own Hands: A People's History of the Grenadian Revolution* and with Danny Reilly of *Telling the Mayflower Story, Thanksgiving or Land Grabbing, Massacres & Slavery?*

Irena Fick was born in London as the daughter of German refugees and is a member of the *Kinder des Widerstands North Rhine-Westfalia*. She lives in London and co-edits the Newsletter of the *Older Feminist Network* and does the research for the *London Socialist Film Co-op*.

Christian Høgsbjerg is Lecturer in Critical History and Politics in the School of Humanities at the University of Brighton. He is the author of *C.L.R. James in Imperial Britain, Chris Braithwaite: Mariner, Renegade and Castaway* and co-author of *Toussaint Louverture: A Black Jacobin in the Age of Revolutions*. He is a member of the editorial board of *International Socialism*.

Merilyn Moos is currently involved in a German organisation for the descendants of survivors, is the author of different books relating to Nazism and is working on a follow-up more detailed study on resistance to the Nazis across Europe which should be published in a couple of years.

Jonathan North is an independent researcher specializing in the Napoleonic era. His most recent books examine Nelson's crimes at Naples (*Nelson at Naples: Revolution and Retribution in 1799*) and the royalist attempt to assassinate Napoleon in 1800 (*Killing Napoleon: The Plot to Blow Up Bonaparte*). His research interests can be found at www.jpnorth.co.uk

Pádraig Óg Ó Ruairc has a PhD in Modern Irish History and has published several books on the Irish Revolution of 1916 - 1923. He can be contacted by e-mail at padraigoruairc@gmail.com and would appreciate any additional information on British men who served in the IRA during the 1916 Rising, Irish War of Independence or Civil War.

Irene Recksiek works for an anti-nuclear movement and is involved in 'anti right-wing' activities. She is also a member of the *Vereinigung der Verfolgten des Naziregimes – Bund der Antifaschistinnen und Antifaschisten* (VVN-BdA, Association of Persecutees of the Nazi Regime/Federation of Antifascists).

David Rovics is a singer/songwriter based in Portland, Oregon. He tours regularly, playing for audiences large and small at cafes, pubs, universities, churches, union halls and protest rallies. His essays are published regularly in *CounterPunch* and *Truthout* and the 200+ songs he makes available on the web have been downloaded more than a million times.

The Socialist History Society

The Socialist History Society was founded in 1992 and includes many leading Socialist and labour historians, academic and amateur researchers, in Britain and overseas. The SHS holds regular events, public meeting controversies. We produce a range of publications, including the journal Socialist History and a regular Newsletter.

The SHS is the successor to the Communist Party History Group, which was established in 1946 and is now totally independent of all political parties and groups. We are engaged in and seek to encourage historical studies from a Marxist and broadly-defined left perspective. We are interested in all aspects of human history from the earliest social formations to the present day and aim for an international approach.

We are particularly interested in the various struggles of labour, of women, of progressive campaigns and peace movements around the world, as well as the history of colonial peoples, black people, and all oppressed communities seeking justice, human dignity and liberation.

Each year we produce two issues of our journal Socialist History, one or two historical pamphlets in our Occasional Publications series, and frequent members' Newsletters. We hold public lectures and seminars mainly in London. In addition, we hold special conferences, book launches and joint events with other friendly groups.

Join the Socialist History Society today!

Members receive all our serial publications for the year at no extra cost and regular mailings about our activities. Members can vote at our AGM and seek election to positions on the committee, and are encouraged to participate in other society activities.

Annual membership fees for 2019 (renewable every January):

Full UK £30.00
Concessionary UK £25.00
Europe full £35.00
Europe concessionary £30.00
Rest of world full £40.00
Rest of world concessionary £35.00

For details of institutional subscriptions, please e-mail the treasurer on francis@socialisthistorysociety.co.uk.

To join the society for 2019, please send your name and address plus a cheque/PO payable to Socialist History Society to: SHS, 50 Elmfield Road, Balham, London SW17 SAL. You can also pay online.

Visit our websites on www.socialisthistorysociety.co.uk and www.lwbooks.co.uk/socialist-history